SPATIAL STRATEGIES
FOR
INTERIOR DESIGN

IAN HIGGINS

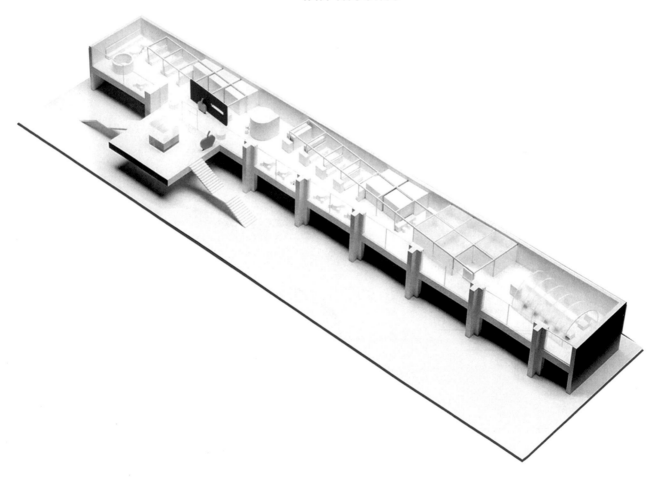

Laurence King Publishing

Contents

Related study material is available on the Laurence King website at **www.laurenceking.com**

Introduction

There are many views as to what interior design is – in this book, the discipline is considered as a specialist three-dimensional design activity, related to, but distinct from, architecture. The interior designer transforms existing buildings to improve their performance or to allow them to be reinvented for a new use. A key aspect of this work is the treatment of the existing envelope and the strategy for the introduction of new elements into the existing space. Inevitably, the interior is a more temporary entity than the architectural envelope it sits in. It is sometimes designed to last only for a few days and occasionally conceived to last for decades. As the discipline we recognize today, interior design is relatively new and so the theory and practice of the subject are less well documented than those of the related disciplines of architecture and furniture design. Traditionally the architect created buildings in which rooms were defined by walls that formed the structure. This resulted in buildings that were, in spatial terms, 'finished' by the architect. If further work was required, an interior *decorator* may have added a veneer of colour, pattern and texture to existing walls, ceilings and floors before selecting and arranging furniture to allow the space to function for its given purpose.

What is interior design?

Interior design is concerned with creating an interface between people and the buildings they use. As a result, the interior designer has to consider a number of issues that range from the strategic to the detailed. The choice of materials touched by the user, the ergonomic qualities of a door handle, creating appropriate acoustic conditions and establishing atmospheric lighting environments are all part of the interior designer's work. Crucial to the success of any interior scheme is the spatial organization of the

Left
This student project proposed converting a nineteenth-century public swimming pool into a place where people could discuss their different religious beliefs. The model shows how the central multifaith prayer space would sit within the drained pool area, its cylindrical shape defined by 360 vertical panels arranged in a radial form. When located at the centre of the drum, users would be able to see through only a single slot at any one time, allowing them to orientate themselves in whichever direction their faith required. This proposal resolves a redundant architectural space while meeting a variety of people's needs, and also succeeds in creating a stimulating spatial experience.

facilities needed to enable the interior to satisfy its functional requirements. In simple terms, this can be referred to as 'planning' and for some projects it might involve the relatively straightforward task of arranging workspaces in a workplace environment or tables and chairs in a restaurant. In reality, however, planning is much more strategic than this. Far from being a 'two-dimensional' activity in which spaces are arranged on plan, it should be thought of as a truly three-dimensional challenge that involves considering: volume and form; the proportion, proximity and relationship of spaces; and the way in which they are articulated, defined and connected as well as the circulation between, through and around them. All these elements have to be developed while managing to satisfy the needs of the interior's users and responding to the constraints established by the existing space in which the interior scheme is to reside. The interior can be regarded as the interface between the building and its users, enabling it to work for a given purpose.

Modernism and the free plan

An argument can be made that the interiors discipline as we understand it today can trace its roots back to the development of Modernism in architecture, and the opportunities this presented for the interior to be considered as an element that could be configured separately from the architectural structure. When Le Corbusier developed his proposal for the mass-production prototype Maison Dom-Ino, in 1914, he suggested a new structural model, with reinforced concrete floor slabs supported by concrete columns set back from the structure's perimeter. By divorcing the building's structure from the walls enclosing it he created a new architecture in which the building's envelope could be hung from the structure like a curtain. This radical idea allowed for a new evaluation of the resulting interior space and the development of his *plan libre* (free plan). With the building structure relying on relatively slender columns and the

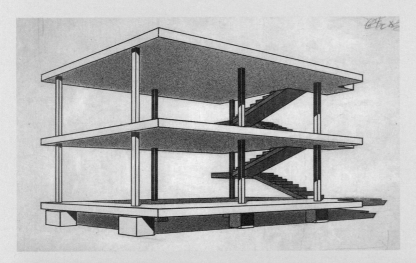

Left
The structural proposal of Le Corbusier's Maison Dom-Ino (1914) consists of concrete floor slabs supported by columns set back from the perimeter, leaving empty space in need of definition to satisfy functional needs within the interior.

Below
In Mies van der Rohe's Concert Hall Project (1942), horizontal and vertical planes are suspended from the host building to create a spatial composition. Each plane is freed from structural responsibility and has the sole purpose of defining volume in which interior activities can take place.

problem of weatherproofing resolved by the concrete slabs and curtain walling, Le Corbusier created an architectural model where the architect could establish an interior volume that was left 'unfinished' in terms of providing specific spaces catering for the precise needs of the building's end user.

The idea that a building's interior space could be 'unfinished' allows the notion of flexibility and change to be considered and offers an opportunity for specialists to emerge who could reconcile the envelope defining the interior space with the needs of the building's users. Freed from having to deal with wider issues concerning topography, structural engineering and weatherproofing, a new breed of specialist interior designers could focus on the task of inhabiting empty architectural space and making it work for the end user.

Ludwig Mies van der Rohe's work in the mid-twentieth century is, arguably, a second important factor in the emergence of interior design as an established discipline in its own right. Influenced by Le Corbusier's thinking,

Mies brought the ideas of the Bauhaus to the United States in the late 1930s. Mid-century America provided a commercial context for European ideas to be put into practice, while in his conceptual projects, Mies explored how flexible interior spaces could be established through compositions of non-structural horizontal and vertical planes housed in architectural superstructures. Again, the interior elements are related to and housed in the architectural envelope while remaining a separate entity.

In 1958, Mies completed his first office building, the Seagram Building on Park Avenue in New York. With this building he put into practice many ideas that he had investigated in previous projects. For interior designers it is significant inasmuch as it presents the quintessential office building, in which the architect has created 39 floors with spaces ready for the interior designer to organize to the precise requirements of the occupants – a task that requires skills distinct from those of the architect.

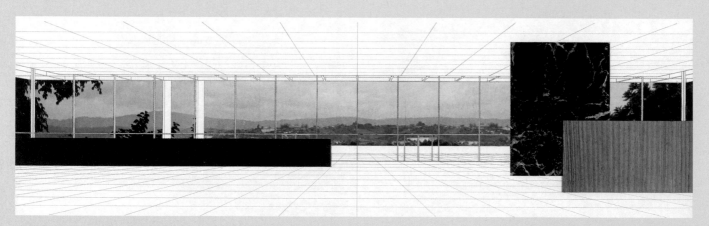

Above
In this proposal drawing for the Bacardi Office Building in Santiago de Cuba, Cuba (1957) by Mies van der Rohe, the interior space is defined by a series of vertical planes.

Below
These plans of the Seagram Building (1958) in New York, USA, show, on the left, the 'unfinished' shell of the building that was designed by Mies van der Rohe and, on the

right, an example of a floor occupied by an end user – in this case, Mercedes-Benz North America, whose office space was created by Selldorf Architects.

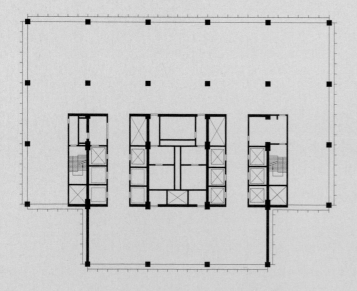

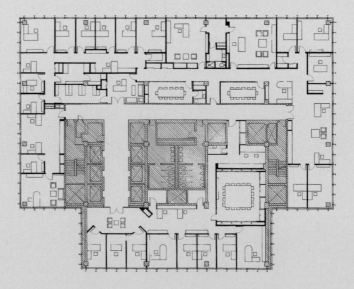

About this book

The following ten chapters aim to simplify the complex problems of planning and organizing compositions of interior spaces by introducing key issues for interior designers to consider during the design process.

Chapter 1: **Points of departure** establishes how, when organizing the planning strategies for interior projects, the contemporary interior designer can start from a variety of different concerns that may include the qualities of the existing site to be used for the project, the function of the proposed interior or the client's ethos.

Chapter 2: **The use of precedent studies** emphasizes the importance of learning from examples of previous good practice to inform future design proposals.

Chapter 3: **Developing conceptual ideas** shows how design decisions can be determined by a clear, bold conceptual direction that may establish the form of the interior while also establishing a narrative that engages the user's interest.

Chapter 4: **Planning strategies** introduces approaches to the development of interior space planning. Spatial strategies, spatial relationships and circulation strategies are identified and explained with the help of appropriate case studies.

Chapter 5: **From brief to proposal** sets out methods of translating the client's needs into an organization of appropriate spaces that reconcile the functional requirements of the brief with the form of the building in which the proposed interior is to be housed.

Chapter 6: **The existing building's impact** demonstrates how the nature of the existing building can be one of the major factors that determine the approach taken towards the establishment of the new interior. Strategies for analyzing existing buildings are outlined and approaches to the introduction of new elements into existing spaces are explained.

Chapter 7: **Developing three-dimensional spatial compositions** demonstrates ways in which it is possible to develop a huge variety of three-dimensional forms from any given planning diagram. Model-making strategies are explained, illustrating how the same plan can deliver many contrasting spatial compositions.

Chapter 8: **Designing in section** emphasizes the importance of an interior's section as a crucial aspect of its design. How the form of an existing building's section can be analyzed, understood and utilized is considered, along with opportunities for the development of the new interior's form in section.

Chapter 9: **Communicating spatial organizations** illustrates the ways in which interior designers use a variety of different methods to communicate complex spatial issues to colleagues, clients and members of the design team. Diagrammatic, orthographic and freehand drawing types as well as models are discussed.

Chapter 10: **What next?** discusses the ensuing stages of the design process once the spatial composition of a project is established. The chapter outlines the process of developing the plan in more detail to satisfy precise functional needs, leading to the detailed design stage and, ultimately, the built reality.

CHAPTER 1
POINTS OF DEPARTURE

Introduction

It is possible to start an interior design project from a number of different departure points, each of which can inform the scheme's planning configuration in different ways. The principal starting points for most design projects are:

- **The existing site**
- **The client**
- **The building programme**

All projects have a client of some kind. A private individual may commission a small residential project and expect the resulting interior to be tailored to their specific needs and requirements. At the other end of the spectrum, a gigantic global corporation might commission a number of interiors around the world. Though these circumstances are vastly different, a common denominator is that both clients require an interior that reflects their particular ethos. Developing a thorough understanding of the client can be the starting point for projects where the built outcome must reflect their values.

The interior designer's work usually takes place within some form of context – generally an existing building whose size, form, materials and construction type can contribute to how the new spaces are organized. In some circumstances, the existing site can be the prime influence on the development of the building plan.

Interiors are formed to create spaces for people to undertake particular functions: the use or 'building programme' will dictate what spaces the scheme requires and how they must relate to each other. For many programmes, there are tried and tested planning formats the interior designer can employ, but there are occasions when developing new ways of delivering a particular use will lead to an original approach to an interior's spatial organization. Whatever the situation, the interior designer will need to consider the building programme when planning the organization of an interior.

Depending on the project, an interior design proposal will often be informed by all these concerns. This chapter will consider the various approaches an interior designer might take to originate a spatial strategy that is appropriate for the constraints and opportunities of the project at hand.

The existing site

The site in which an interior is to be created will usually present a number of opportunities and constraints that can be major factors in determining the planning approach. Some of the existing site qualities that could inform the strategy for a scheme's spatial organization include:

- **The site's history**
- **The existing cellular spaces**
- **The structural grid**
- **The form of the building's section**

Below
Architectural practice group8 created their offices in a former industrial building near Geneva, Switzerland in 2010. In response to the site's history, the interior is conceived as a storage facility, leading to a spatial composition defined by shipping containers placed in the space.

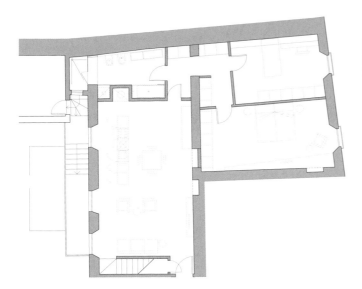

Above

In 2012, Archiplan Studio designed this small apartment in Mantova, Italy. The existing building consisted of two well-established volumes defined by thick, load-bearing brick walls, and the established cellular spaces determined the opportunities for the new scheme's spatial organization.

Above

The White Cube Gallery in Bermondsey, London, UK was fashioned out of a 1970s warehouse building by Casper Mueller Kneer Architects in 2011. Three distinct gallery spaces were created, along with an auditorium, private viewing rooms, a bookshop and warehousing. The existing structural grid determined the organization of the spaces.

1 Entrance
2 Bookshop
3 North galleries
4 Auditorium
5 South galleries
6 9x9x9
7 Viewing rooms
8 Archive
9 Meeting room

Case study The existing site

Trace Architecture Office, Beijing, China / Trace Architecture

Trace Architecture Office reused a redundant aeronautical factory in northern Beijing to create a studio workspace for their practice in 2009. The resulting scheme was driven by the qualities of the existing site.

In spatial terms, the existing building was configured from four identical rectangular bays organized to form two distinct parts. The entrance zone was made up of two bays with a ceiling height of 4 metres (13 feet) placed end to end, and this 'tunnel' led to the second area, where two bays were placed side by side to form a large cubic volume with a ceiling height of close to 8 metres (26 feet).

The proposal responds to these spatial conditions by inserting a new element housing most of the studio's support facilities within the initial linear space. Arranged over two floors, this object introduces a mezzanine level that creates low-ceilinged spaces and, as it occupies half the width of the space, accentuates its tunnel-like qualities. Grouping the ancillary functions into this zone leaves the large cubic volume free to play host to the studio space. The contrast established between the constrained route and the expansive destination creates drama.

The interior scheme also responds to the existing site in terms of the materials used. Layers of decoration were stripped from the host building to reveal a raw industrial aesthetic defined by concrete, steel and timber – the site history acts as a counterpoint to the clean lines of the new elements made of white-painted plasterboard, frosted glass and vinyl. This results in a scheme where a smooth new object sits within a robust and heavily textured shell.

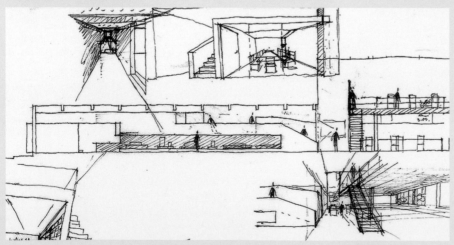

Above left and above
A built object placed in the entrance zone houses support facilities. This new element further constrains the proportions of the space, emphasizing its tunnel-like qualities.

Left
Early sketch drawings explore the spatial idea of functions being grouped within a linear box that is 'parked' in the initial long and low space.

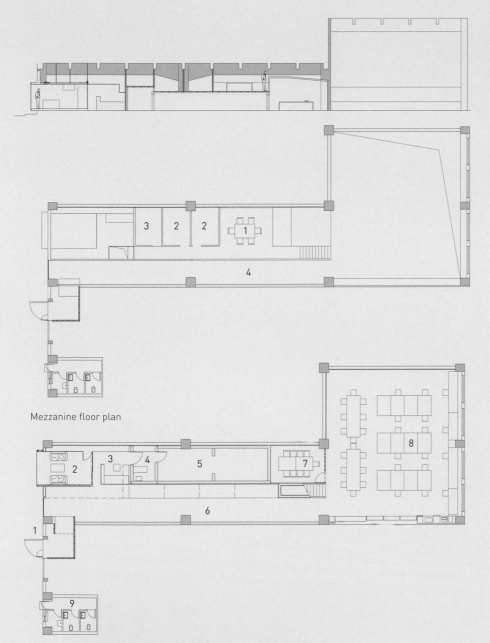

Mezzanine floor plan

Mezzanine floor plan

Ground floor plan

Left
The plan and section drawings of the scheme show how the proposal exploits the site's spatial qualities. Support facilities are constrained within the low, narrow volume, allowing the studio to occupy the large open space.

1   Work area
2   Office
3   Tea room
4   Void

1   Entry
2   Lounge
3   Reception
4   Office
5   Storage
6   Gallery
7   Meeting room
8   Work area
9   Bathroom

Left
The scheme responds to the existing site in material terms: new elements are smooth and white, in contrast to the dark, textured and raw existing materials.

The client

Most interior design work involves creating spaces to support some form of commercial activity and, as such, will be instigated by a client. In some circumstances, the client may simply wish to create an interior that is appropriate for the particular use and site concerned. For example, a manufacturer of pharmaceutical products may need to set up an administrative office at its factory: in this instance, the requirement may be for an interior solution that provides a workspace that reconciles the functional requirements with the existing building. There are also occasions when a client requires an interior solution that embodies their identity, ethos or aspirations, and in these circumstances the project can be driven by the client's identity.

Below

Google, an American multinational corporation, creates informal, playful and relaxed workspaces for its employees, with the intention of encouraging creative activity. In the UK, the company has established Campus, a co-working space in east London's burgeoning 'Tech City' that offers flexible workspace for start-up companies. Google commissioned Jump Studios to design the interior (completed in 2012) and though it is a deliberately 'unbranded' space, the scheme incorporates many of the ideas pioneered in Google's own corporate offices. The building was stripped back to its core to establish a raw environment, similar to a garage or workshop, and new elements are made of inexpensive, utilitarian materials. Together, they form spaces designed to reflect the personalities of the young start-up companies that will use the building. The intention is that this workplace will be very different from that of an established, corporate company and as such will embody the values Google wishes to communicate.

Right

The consumer electronics, personal computers and software produced by the American multinational corporation Apple Inc. have a reputation for technical innovation coupled with intuitive, user-friendly design that has an understated, elegant simplicity. A consistent corporate philosophy pervades all aspects of the organization's activities.

Below left and right

Since the first Apple Store opened in 2001, the chain of retail outlets owned by Apple Inc. has grown to more than 400 units in 14 countries. The stores are incredibly successful: in terms of sales per unit area, they are often the most profitable retail environments in their locations. Originally conceived by Apple CEO Steve Jobs in conjunction with designers Eight Inc., the interiors manage to embody the attributes of Apple products. A straightforward plan clarifies the shopping experience and a restrained palette of materials is elegantly detailed to create an apparently simple space where the products are paramount. In addition, the shopping process is reinvented: visitors can freely use products without making purchases and new technology is engaged to turn each member of the shop-floor team into a mobile purchase point. This strategy transforms the traditional planning requirements of a retail space.

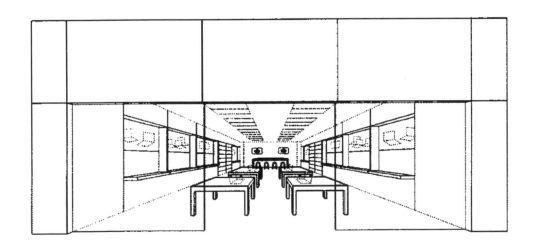

Left

In 2013, Apple Inc. registered a trademark for the Apple Store design. The glass shopfront, panelled facade, rectangular recessed lighting to the ceiling, recessed wall spaces with cantilevered shelves, rectangular wooden tables and an oblong bench at the rear of the space, set beneath video screens, are all cited as elements that, when arranged in a particular way, define an Apple Store. This drawing sets out the criteria for the trademark.

Case study The client

DAKS, London, UK / Alex Nevedomskis (Kingston University, UK)

This 2011 student project developed design proposals for a flagship menswear store for the British fashion brand DAKS. Many of the design decisions made on this project were driven by an understanding of the client.

The DAKS name has long been synonymous with British heritage, style and elegance. Originally founded in 1894, the brand is now a quintessentially British luxury label, specializing in fine tailoring and accessories for both men and women. The unique 'House Check' was introduced in 1976 and has become an international symbol for the brand. It features heavily throughout the company's clothing and accessories ranges.

Located on London's Piccadilly, the shop sits between Jermyn Street and Savile Row, both of which are associated with gentleman's tailoring. The building was designed by the British architect Edwin Lutyens in 1922 and, as a former bank, its interior has many traditional elements including timber wall panelling, parquet flooring and ornate ceiling details that help establish a masculine environment appropriate for the brand's heritage. The old banking hall presents a double-height cubic volume topped by a ceiling that is defined as a nine-square grid. These site qualities facilitated the introduction of a new mezzanine level whose square, gridded form references the client's 'House Check' fabric. The dimensions of these new 'bespoke' elements are tailor-made for the site and the new floor level organizes the section of the building to create a traditional ground-floor space (lined with dark timber) and a modern light-filled mezzanine above. The contrasting spaces allude to the company's history and its reinvention as a contemporary fashion brand.

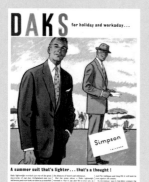
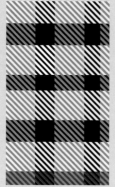

Far left
Founded in 1894, DAKS was a major British fashion label throughout the twentieth century.

Centre
Introduced in 1976, the DAKS 'House Check' is a key symbol of the brand and features heavily in its clothing and accessories ranges.

Left
Recent collections have created a range of contemporary clothing that captures the spirit of the brand's heritage.

Left
The organization of the proposal involved the insertion of a new 'tailor-made' floor to create a modern mezzanine level above a traditional ground-floor space. The form of the new elements responds to the site geometry (as expressed in the ornate ceiling) and the DAKS 'House Check' pattern.

The building programme

The spatial organization of most interior design projects is driven by the building's function or 'building programme'. It is essential for the scheme to provide the spaces necessary for the activities concerned and to ensure that they are arranged in an appropriate manner to facilitate the particular use. While it may be important for the scheme to respond to the opportunities presented by the site context and to express the client's ethos, ultimately the interior must work for the people who use it. The same core use can often be accommodated in a variety of ways and this will result in very different floor plans that provide users with completely different experiences. It is the interior designer's job to choreograph the visitor's use of the interior to provide an appropriate experience.

Restaurants provide a straightforward building programme that can be organized in a number of different ways, depending on the circumstances. Many factors influence the planning of a restaurant: more expensive restaurants generally provide more space for each diner; seating arrangements are manipulated to create a different ambience; and a number of systems can be utilized to order and serve food, including waiter service, self-service and assisted service. Each serving strategy requires a different planning arrangement, which is driven by the precise nature of the specific building programme. Above all, restaurants are interesting environments in that they must seamlessly combine the customer's relaxing leisure environment with the staff's busy workplace. For a restaurant to succeed, the interior must meet the needs of both these groups.

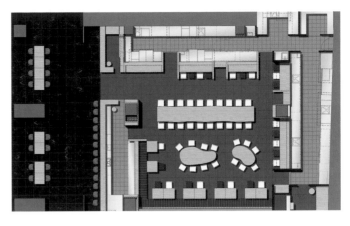

Above
Ippudo is a Japanese noodle restaurant in Sydney, Australia completed in 2012 by Koichi Takada Architects. The interior's plan is driven by the building programme: the staff areas (kitchen, reception and bar) are arranged in a 'U' shape, wrapping around the site to leave a square dining area in the middle. The planning of the dining space is determined by a variety of different seating arrangements that offer customers a choice of experience – banquette seating, a communal refectory table and informal groupings of seats placed around shared lozenge-shaped tables are all integrated within the scheme.

Below
In 2009, Andres Remy Arquitectos completed Get & Go, a takeaway restaurant in Buenos Aires, Argentina. The building programme responds to the restaurant's name and dictates the planning, so that customers are processed through an efficient sequence of events in order to 'get' and 'go'. Customers enter on the right-hand side of the shop and circulate around a servery placed in the middle of the front space – this acts as an island they must pass around, where they can order and pay for coffee and food. Next a waiting area is provided before customers collect their food and exit through the other glass door. A third (opaque) door provides separate staff access to the kitchen at the rear.

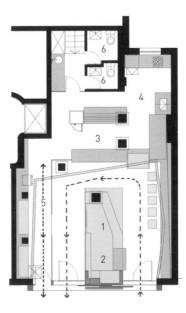

1 Cashier
2 Café
3 Counter
4 Kitchen
5 Delivery area
6 Bathroom

Left

In 2012, Integrated Field created Coca Grill, a restaurant in Bangkok, Thailand specializing in Asian street food. In response to this building programme, the designers developed a dining module that captures the essence of a street vendor's cart and these modules were then arranged in the interior. The spatial organization is the result of their installation.

Left and below

This restaurant and bookshop scheme is located in a museum and cultural centre in the Spanish city of Santiago de Compostela. Completed by Estudio Nômada in 2010, the interior is conceived as a collection of large-scale furniture elements, each of which delivers a function identified by the building programme. A long servery acts as the bar and shop counter, a cylindrical volume creates an office space and two refectory tables are placed under abstracted tree structures that allude to communal gatherings at outdoor festivals in the region. They are set in a temporary way, with the intention that the restaurant elements do not interfere with the architectural envelope.

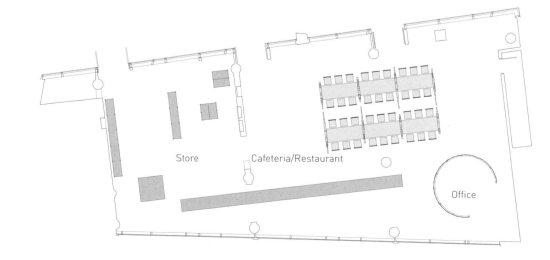

Store   Cafeteria/Restaurant   Office

Case study The building programme

Sushi-teria restaurant, New York, USA / form-ula

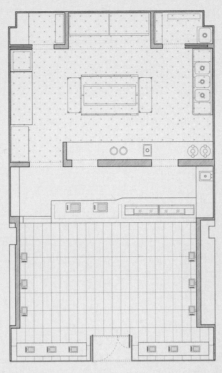

Located in a commercial office development in New York, Sushi-teria is a small takeaway restaurant serving made-to-order sushi that opened in 2012. The outlet's innovative ordering technology has an impact on the interior planning: customers use touchscreens and an app to place their orders. This results in an arrangement where approximately half the space is allocated to the kitchen, with the remainder of the plan consisting of the customer-ordering area and the servery. Due to the ordering system, the counter's functions are reduced to payment and food collection, facilitating a more efficient service.

Above
The programme for the restaurant introduces a digital ordering process that informs the plan of the customer space: the organization establishes clarity of purpose while at the same time maximizing the number of terminals within this zone.

Below
The store is designed with great clarity, and the fully glazed shopfront gives passers-by an unimpeded view of the interior.

Left
The simple, clear plan is divided into three distinct adjacent spaces: the kitchen, the servery and the customer zone. The new digital ordering system means that the counter zone becomes more efficient, as its functions are reduced to payment and food collection.

CHAPTER 2
THE USE OF PRECEDENT STUDIES

Introduction

Interior design work is rarely undertaken in isolation – the occasional project may require the designer to develop a response to a whole new building programme or a set of unprecedented circumstances, but usually designers learn from that which has gone before. Precedent is concerned with the use of previous examples to inform and justify a similar design decision when comparable circumstances arise. Young designers are often obsessed with originality and believe that it is essential to create proposals that are new and without precedent. In reality this is a rather unrealistic and unhelpful approach – buildings have been designed for thousands of years and interior designers should understand that this is the context in which they undertake their work. Many design projects will simply operate within the established boundaries of the subject, others will contribute to its evolution and development, while a few may ultimately revolutionize and redefine the way in which the discipline is performed.

Precedent examples can be used to inform and justify any aspect of the design process, from a building's entrance sequence through to the language of detailing, material selection and furniture specification. When considering the spatial organization of a design scheme, precedent studies might help the designer establish appropriate strategies for the introduction of a new element to a given site, the organization of spaces or the circulation strategies used to connect them to each other.

Coupled with an obsessive preoccupation with contemporary practice, the development of a wide and in-depth knowledge of the history of interior design, architecture and related disciplines can only be of benefit to an interior designer, allowing them to make informed decisions that enhance the project. This chapter will look at ways in which precedent studies can be used to inform the development of design proposals, with particular reference to the spatial organization of an interior.

Learning from history

Designers have always referred to that which has gone before, but it is perhaps important to develop an awareness of the difference between 'referencing' or 'quoting from' the past and blindly copying the work of other designers. The history of interior design is closely entwined with the history of architecture, and it is often possible to trace the historical roots of a particular scheme by making connections between a number of projects that together create a 'family tree' of work exploring a particular theme or idea. In these circumstances each 'project generation' might add value by taking the idea further or launching it in a different direction, to be pursued by others at a later date.

Above
Mies van der Rohe's sketch for a Glass House on a Hillside (c.1934) explores the idea of a house as a rectilinear volume that floats above a sloping site.

Below and bottom
Mies van der Rohe's proposal informs the concept for a Zip-up House (1968) by Richard Rogers, in which the form is developed to become a solid tube with a glazed end.

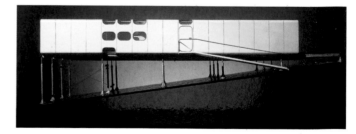

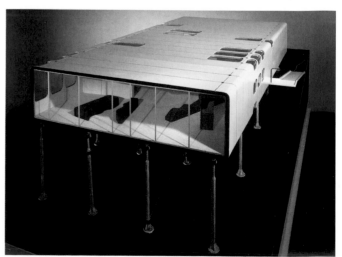

Above
The Zip-up House concept then forms the basis for the 1969 house Richard and Su Rogers built for his parents in south-west London, UK. This seminal house has in turn influenced a number of subsequent buildings.

Right
It is difficult to imagine Foster + Partners' 1978 Sainsbury Centre for Visual Arts in Norwich, UK (shown here in a section diagram) without referring to the precedent of the Rogers House in London.

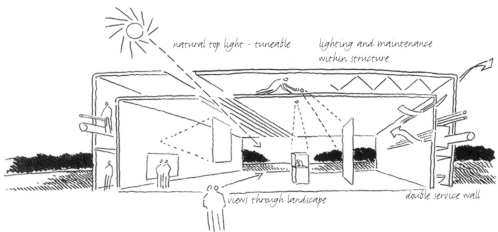

natural top light - tuneable

lighting and maintenance within structure

views through landscape

double service wall

Site precedents

A project site will often have particular qualities that present distinct challenges for the interior designer. This might involve the building type (the reuse of a church, for example), the construction type (a vernacular timber construction), the building's form (a round building) or its condition (raising questions regarding approaches to conservation, restoration or refurbishment). In these circumstances an awareness of previous responses to the particular issue can be an important contributing factor to the solution.

Far left

This industrial laundry in south-west London, UK was used as the site for a student project, as its existing condition presented an opportunity to consider how the redundant machinery could be incorporated into the student's proposals. There are many precedents that can inform work in this context.

Left

In 1997 Foster + Partners completed a project in Essen, Germany that transformed the powerhouse building of an early twentieth-century coal-mining complex into a design centre. Much of the project was concerned with conserving and restoring the existing building, and many of the building's industrial elements were retained to contrast with the newly introduced interior. The scheme establishes a bold approach for work in existing buildings with an industrial heritage.

Left

An old steelworks in Rotherham, UK was transformed into Magna, a 'science adventure centre'. Completed in 2001 by Wilkinson Eyre Architects, the scheme defines an approach to working in redundant industrial spaces: large new pavilions appear to 'float' in an existing site that is seemingly untouched.

Organization precedents

Interiors can be organized using a number of different methods, including linear, radial, clustered and grid strategies. Many designers have used these tactics on many occasions to solve many organizational requirements. An awareness of approaches that have been used in the past can help inform design decisions today and allow an interior designer to progress a scheme with confidence.

In addition to the approach taken for the layout and organization of spaces, the methods used to define and differentiate between spaces will be of great importance. Much can be learned from previous examples about the most appropriate strategies for a given project.

Below
In the early 1920s, the Dutch designer Theo van Doesburg was a founding member of the De Stijl movement, whose members pioneered the idea of space being defined by a composition of intersecting planes. This method of establishing space has had an important impact on the development of interior design.

Below
Stefan Zwicky designed an exhibition stand for carpet manufacturer Melchnau at the Heimtextil trade show in Frankfurt, Germany in 1993. The installation is a composition of overlapping vertical planes that is rooted in the work of van Doesburg.

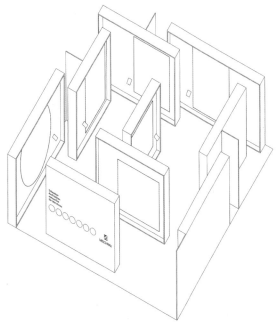

Left
Completed by i29 in 2012, the Combiwerk 'social workplace' in the Dutch city of Delft is a composition of vertical planes and bold colours – an approach that has its origins in the work of van Doesburg.

Case study Spatial precedents: a space within a space

Glass House, New Canaan, USA / Philip Johnson

Philip Johnson's Glass House is a seminal building of the twentieth century. Completed in 1949, it has a number of attributes that have led to it's being regarded as one of the most significant buildings of the period.

Johnson is credited with being instrumental in introducing European Modernism to the United States. He described the building as 'a clearing house of ideas which can filter down later, through my own work or that of others', and as such it could be seen as a deliberate attempt to establish a number of precedents to be explored by future designers. In the Glass House, Johnson realized a number of early preoccupations that have gone on to influence the work of many designers.

Right
The cylindrical form contains the hearth, toilet, washbasin and shower. It is placed like an object on the floor plan, carefully positioned to help define the zones established in the open volume that remains.

Below
From the approach, the building can clearly be understood as a transparent rectangular box housing a solid cylindrical form.

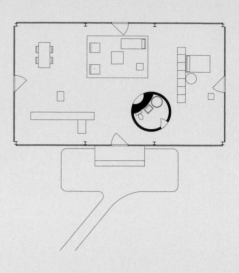

Above
A cylindrical room was created to read as a 'space within a space' when John Pawson's 'Plain Space' exhibition was installed at the Fondazione Bisazza in Vicenza, Italy in 2012.

Below
The meeting room in this office building in Tianjin, China was conceived as a curvilinear 'space within a space' by Vector Architects (2012).

These preoccupations include:

- The use of an **elevated base plane** on which the building is placed
- The establishment of an **overhead plane** to define the volume
- The **transparent envelope** blurring boundaries between inside and outside
- The **open-plan** organization of the interior

Perhaps the greatest precedent set by this building is the idea of a '**space within a space**'. This strategy is particularly effective at the Glass House because the whole building programme is housed in two volumes, creating a spatial composition of exceptional clarity. This is further emphasized by the manner in which the spaces are articulated in terms of form and material – a transparent glass box holds a solid brick cylinder. Many interior designers have been able to use this approach to great effect in subsequent situations.

Circulation precedents

When developing the planning and spatial organization for a building, the circulation strategy employed will be of particular importance. This could involve considering the relationship of circulation routes to the spaces they serve, or the way in which the circulation pathway is defined or articulated. An understanding of how leading designers and architects have tackled similar issues in the past will provide a valuable insight as to how to develop a solution for a project at hand.

Below left

In the early 1960s, Carlo Scarpa was commissioned to refurbish the ground floor of the Querini Stampalia Foundation, a museum housed in a sixteenth-century Venetian palace. The building had been repeatedly flooded and Scarpa inserted a new raised floor in the main exhibition space. Where the floor spills out into the adjacent spaces it can be read as a 'tray' with upstands that can control future floodwater. The scheme introduces new elements into an existing building so that they are 'separate' and 'distinct' and controls circulation by taking visitors on a journey through an existing space without touching it. Many designers have used this approach as a precedent when creating new circulation paths in an existing building.

Below

The 2012 German Pavilion at the Venice Biennale housed an exhibition titled 'Reduce/Reuse/Recycle', designed by Konstantin Grcic. The scheme responded to the site location and the exhibition theme by using *passerelles* (the temporary structures used during high tide to provide dry walkways for pedestrians) to link spaces together. Used in this interior setting, the *passerelles*, which were on loan from the local municipality, reference Scarpa's earlier work.

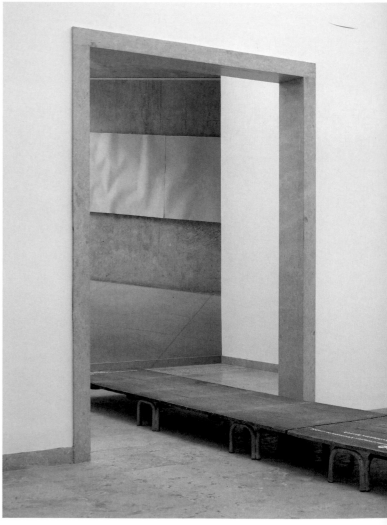

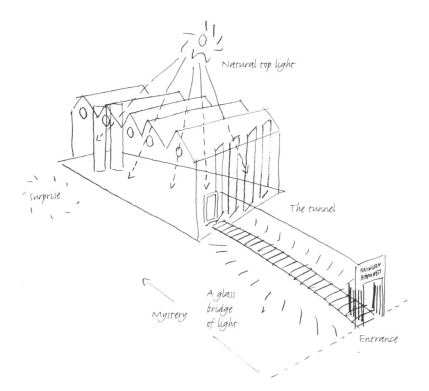

Natural top light

surprise

Mystery

The tunnel

A glass
bridge
of light

Entrance

Left

Left
Foster + Partners' 1987 scheme
for the Katherine Hamnett store
in London, UK had to solve
the problem of how to entice
customers through a rather scruffy
tunnel that took them from the
street to a shop occupying an old
industrial space hidden behind
adjacent buildings. The solution
created a dramatic journey by
introducing a single pristine
element – a glass bridge lit from
below. The gently arching walkway
meandered on plan to deliver
visitors into the retail space. The
way in which the new bridge
relates to the existing architecture
references Scarpa's work.

Left
For their 1992 scheme for the
Dinosaur Gallery at the Natural
History Museum, London, UK
Imagination introduced a new
bridge into the existing double-
height space, allowing visitors to
view large exhibits displayed on
either side. The new steel structure
contrasts with the existing
building's decorative elements.
Scarpa's earlier work informs the
relationship between new and
existing structures, and the way
in which circulation is controlled.

Case study Circulation precedent: a controlled pathway

Ikea and Tiger stores

Ikea aims to bring people well-designed, functional home products at affordable prices. Since opening its first furniture showroom in Älmhult, Sweden in 1953, Ikea has grown into an iconic brand with stores in more than 40 countries. Over the last 60 years, these stores have evolved to become environments with which most people are familiar: typically an out-of-town superstore comprising three retail sections – the 'showroom', the 'marketplace' and the 'warehouse' – and a restaurant. Upon arrival, customers are encouraged to either visit the restaurant or walk through the showroom, where products are displayed in room sets and furniture is grouped in appropriate categories. Upon exiting the showroom, customers are presented with another opportunity to visit the restaurant or they can take a shopping trolley and progress to the marketplace, where they can make their selection from the thousands of smaller products on display. Finally, customers enter the warehouse, where large items are stored close to the checkout area. Circulation within the stores is carefully planned to encourage a one-way flow, forcing customers to journey past all that the store has to offer. Although shortcuts do exist and it is possible to walk against the circulation flow, most people find themselves following others in what is essentially a queue of people. This simple planning idea creates a quite unusual retail environment that has been hugely successful.

Tiger, another Scandinavian company, sets out to offer customers cheap and cheerful products with style, in a fun environment. The Danish retailer operates on a much smaller scale than Ikea and outlets are usually located in typical urban shopping centres. Tiger shops employ a circulation and planning strategy inspired by the Ikea model: display fixtures are used to define a circulation route that takes customers on a one-way journey from entrance to exit, passing all the shop's products on the way.

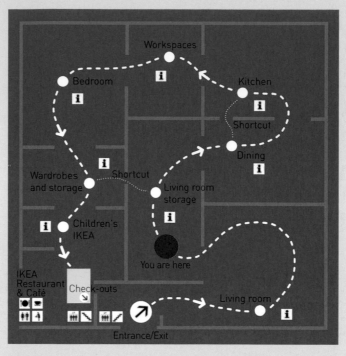

Above
A diagram designed to explain the layout of an Ikea store to customers shows how shoppers are taken through the initial 'showroom' section on a prescribed linear route, through a sequence of zones where furniture is displayed in room sets and by product category.

Below
Although much smaller in scale, Tiger shops employ the same strategy as Ikea: circulation is controlled to create a one-way route that ensures customers see all the products on offer prior to payment and exit.

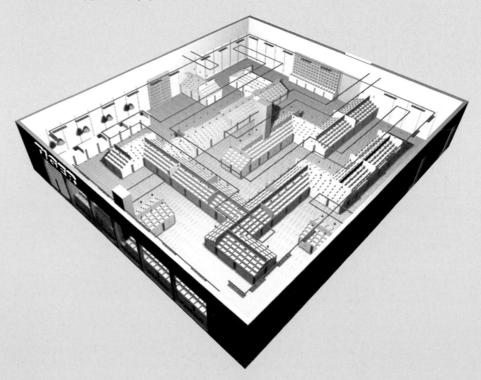

Learning from other disciplines

Naturally it is common for designers to draw precedent studies from examples within the disciplines of interior design and architecture, but there are also many instances where ideas transferred from other disciplines can provide justification for a particular approach. These may come from closely related fields such as furniture design, product design or graphic design, or they could employ thinking from other fields, such as science or nature. Designers will often refer to the art world, citing paintings or sculptures as references for their design decisions.

Left and above
As the leader of the Knoll Planning Unit, in 1951 Florence Knoll designed the furniture company's New York showroom on Madison Avenue. She set out to create an informal spatial composition of overlapping spaces and the influence of Theo van Doesburg's 1929 painting *Simultaneous Composition XXIV* is evident in her scheme. The artist used rectilinear shapes in primary colours to explore the definition of space; this seminal work of the De Stijl movement has influenced many Modernist architects and designers.

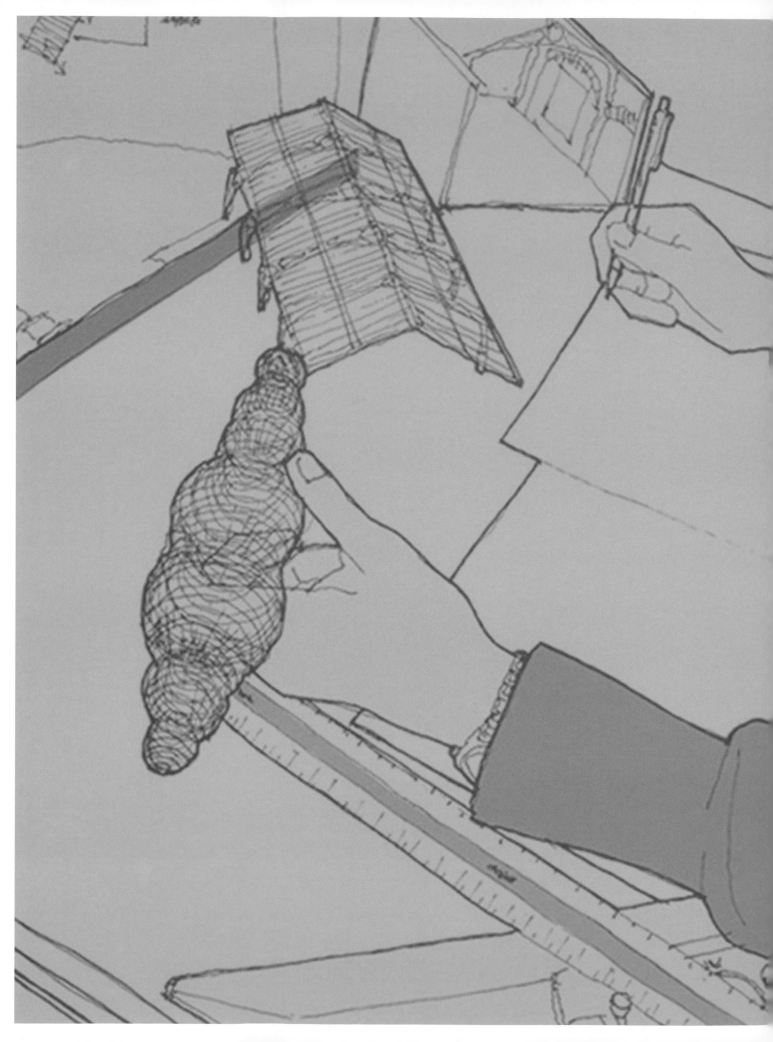

CHAPTER 3
DEVELOPING CONCEPTUAL IDEAS

Introduction

In the first instance, it is necessary for an interior to function well for the activity for which it is designed. It should be taken as given that a professional interior designer will create spaces that work for the end users in practical terms. On top of this, the role of the interior designer might be to create spaces that satisfy more than just the most obvious functional requirements: spaces of great beauty, spaces that meet emotional needs and engage and delight the user, spaces that respond to the existing architecture in interesting and meaningful ways, spaces that tell a story or spaces that reinvent how functional requirements are met and change the way in which people use an interior or undertake an activity.

A good interior will deliver more than a straightforward practical solution and, to this end, an interior design project will often be driven by a big idea that is called 'the concept'. This chapter will identify different types of concepts and the ways in which conceptual ideas might be generated for interior design projects.

What is a concept?

For an interior designer, a concept could be defined as an abstract or general idea that might inform decisions taken during the design process so that the built outcome will be more cohesive. A concept might relate to the whole project and inform all aspects of decision-making, from planning through to detailing and materials specification, or it might be applied to a particular part of the design process, such as a 'planning concept', a 'lighting concept' or a 'colour concept'.

This page
The Oki-ni flagship store on Savile Row in London, UK was completed in 2001 by 6a Architects. The concept for the project was that of a sloping oak tray inserted into a concrete shell, leaving a series of perimeter spaces that could conceal changing rooms and stairs. The fan-shaped tray, which defines the shop floor, acts as an independent element separate from the existing building fabric.

Analogy, ideas and invention

The development of ideas comes naturally to some people, who may then be perceived as having a natural flair for creative thinking. While this may be true, most designers can create interesting and appropriate conceptual directions for projects: ultimately, generating ideas is all about thinking and designers can develop methods of thinking to help them become more confident about their ability to create.

Paul Laseau, an artist and architect, believes that good conceptual ideas emerge as part of the 'discovery process'. He suggests that 'for the designer the process of discovery consists of two parts: *invention and concept formation*. Invention seeks the basic discovery, the original idea for the project; concept formation converts the discovery into a graphic and verbal statement that can give basic direction to the full development of the project.'[1]

Laseau notes that, according to furniture designer David Pye, invention 'can only be done deliberately if the inventor can discern similarities between the particular result which he is envisaging and some other actual result which he has seen and stored in his memory' and that 'an inventor's power to invent depends on his ability to see analogies'.[2] That is to say, in order to develop the skills necessary to generate ideas and concepts for any discipline, a designer needs to be able to make comparisons between two different things that share characteristics. The ability to identify the given aspects of a project, and analyze how any of these components might offer an opportunity to develop ideas that can be manifested in a building, is key to generating useful and creative conceptual ideas within the discipline of interior design. The given aspects of any project may include the site, the planned use, the client, the budget and the lifespan of the proposed interior. Any or all of these issues could be a fertile source of ideas to shape the direction a project takes. For a conceptual idea to be useful, it has to be a tool that helps to make decisions that advance and enhance the project. The big idea underpinning the project should help, not hinder, the proposal.

1 Paul Laseau, *Graphic Thinking for Architects and Designers* (New York, 2001), p. 142.
2 David Pye, *The Nature of Design* (London, 1964), pp. 65–66.

This page
This student project proposed a studio and residence for a sculptor set in a former industrial building. The concept was generated from the idea that an analogy could be made between a chest of drawers and a way of defining interior space. As a result, a thick central wall was introduced to separate the studio from the residence. An early development model shows how the wall was conceived as a gigantic piece of furniture with drawer-like volumes pulled out of it.

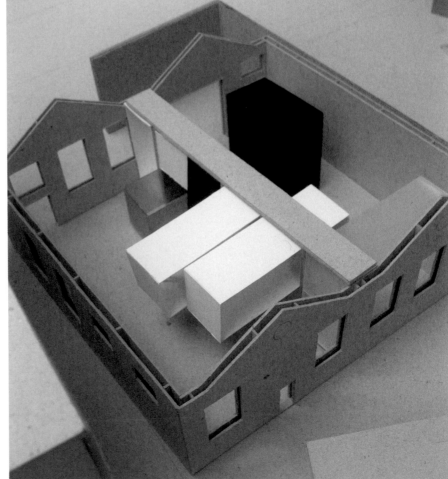

Conceptual starting points

Concepts can be generated from many starting points but for the idea to be clever it is usually best for the proposed direction to have some relevance to the project at hand. When starting work on a proposal, the interior designer can make an appraisal of its component parts to ascertain possible opportunities for a conceptual direction. What is relevant will vary from project to project but can often emerge from the following points of departure:

- **The client**
- **The programme**
- **The site**
- **The design approach**

The conceptual approach to a proposal will often have a number of layers that might draw on a variety of different aspects of the project for inspiration.

Above

Two conceptual ideas underpin Dan Brunn Architects' 2007 scheme for a stone company's showroom in San Francisco, USA. The first was concerned with the treatment of the existing building and the way the new elements relate to this shell (the building's timberwork was sandblasted to provide a raw volume into which the pristine new elements are inserted), while the second was a bold planning approach involving a single element that slices through the building and organizes the activities within.

Right

A diagram explaining the concept shows the building as an empty box that is sliced in two by a new wall that runs its length. All the cellular spaces are grouped together to form 'private' spaces behind the wall, allowing the remaining open space to become the 'public' showroom. The scheme uses the existing trusses as a reference point to locate the interior elements.

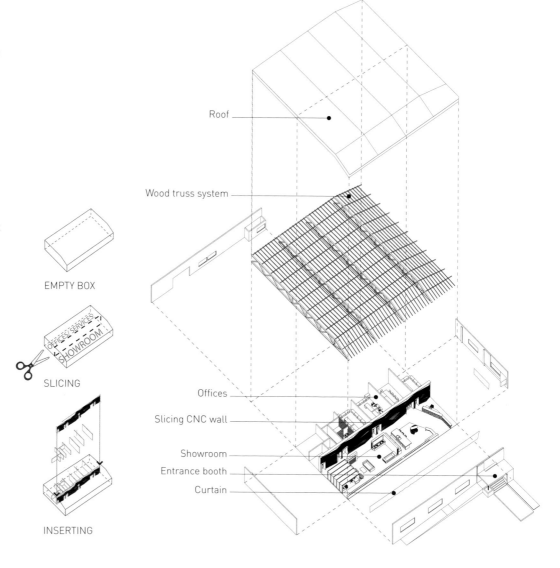

EMPTY BOX

SLICING

INSERTING

Roof

Wood truss system

Offices

Slicing CNC wall

Showroom

Entrance booth

Curtain

Concepts based on the client

There are a number of ways in which a project's client can be the starting point for the scheme's conceptual idea. Commercial projects might draw inspiration from the following sources, among others:

- **The nature of the client's business**
- **The client's products or services**
- **The client's corporate identity**

Residential projects will often be driven by the client's background, their interests or the particular functional requirements they have for their home.

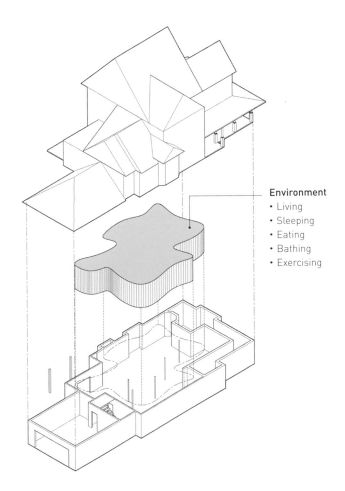

Environment
- Living
- Sleeping
- Eating
- Bathing
- Exercising

Below and below right

In 2010 Dake Wells Architecture completed this office for KLF Architectural Systems, an aluminium window supplier located in a suburban retail centre in Springfield, Missouri, USA. The conceptual direction for the project was derived from the nature of the client's business and the company's use of dies to form extrusions. The office space is conceived as a volume that has been extruded from the solid block of the shopping centre, creating a profiled space whose form references a section through a glazing extrusion.

Right

SIDE Architecture completed this residential scheme in a traditional three-storey suburban house in Chicago, USA in 2010. The clients had lived and travelled in south-east Asia and wished to transplant the character of the eastern way of living into their existing home, so this became the basis for a conceptual idea for the project. A decision was made to keep the two different architectural languages separate from each other, which is why a fluid arrangement of timber screens was introduced on the ground floor as an independent insertion. This diagram illustrates the conceptual relationship between the existing building and the new elements.

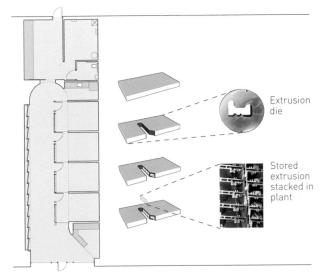

Extrusion die

Stored extrusion stacked in plant

STEP BY STEP DEVELOPING A CONCEPTUAL IDEA

The brief for this student project started with the word 'listen' and a given site. The following drawings explain how the conceptual idea was developed.

1 **Investigation**: the site for the project is a railway station and a decision is made to investigate how the building might provide the conceptual starting point.

2 **Analysis**: the ambient noise of the railway station is recorded and analysis determines that the 'bing bong' tone used to introduce announcements made over the public address system is the quintessential sound of the space.

3 **Invention**: a recording of the tone is analyzed using computer software that transforms the sound into a visual form.

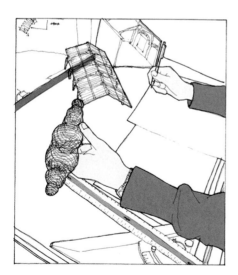

4 **Development**: the two-dimensional representation of the sound is developed into a three-dimensional form, the size of which responds to the existing building structure.

5 **Outcome**: a new type of interactive music store is created as the 'bing bong' tone manifests itself as a blob-like structure that inhabits the site. When a user touches a tile on the rotating faceted form, a piece of music is downloaded to their telephone.

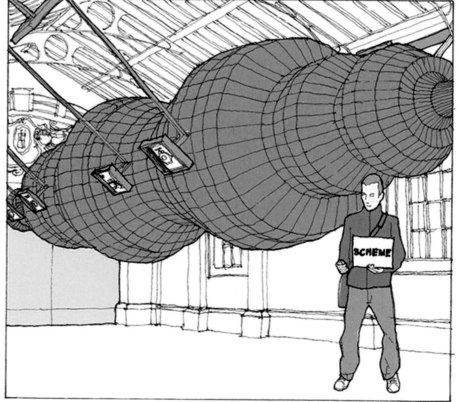

Concepts based on the programme

The project's programme (what the building is used for) can be a rich source of material for the development of conceptual ideas for the spatial organization of interior design schemes. This can often result in a 'narrative' response, where a particular aspect of the activity proposed for the building is used to generate ideas that can provide an agenda for the project. An interior with a narrative element tells a story that users of the building may understand and appreciate – each part of the composition acts as a metaphor to enhance the experience (see case study on page 45).

There are occasions when the way in which a particular programme is delivered is completely re-evaluated and the designer develops a whole new system to deal with the problem at hand. This reinvention of a typology can take the form of a big idea becoming a concept that demands a new approach to the planning and spatial organization of a scheme. An example of this would be Ikea stores, where the accepted notion of a retail space was replaced with an organization that, in simple terms, divides the main activity into three zones: the showroom, the marketplace and the self-service area (see page 32). Customers then navigate the spaces on a linear route that encourages them to experience everything the store has to offer.

This page
For this 2008 scheme in Linz, Austria, x architekten adopted a narrative approach derived from the interior's use as a dental surgery. An analogy was drawn between a dental diagram used to identify teeth and its potential as a building plan, where the space between the upper and lower teeth becomes the circulation zone, the teeth become panels on the partition wall and the numbered rectangles represent the treatment rooms.

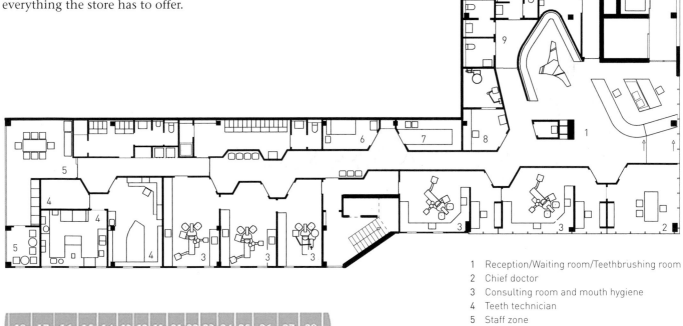

1   Reception/Waiting room/Teethbrushing room
2   Chief doctor
3   Consulting room and mouth hygiene
4   Teeth technician
5   Staff zone
6   Rest room
7   Sterilization
8   Radiography room
9   Patients' room
10 Technician

Concepts based on the site

The qualities of the existing building will often be the source of a conceptual idea that drives a project forward. Concepts that relate to the site might respond to the following issues, among others:

- **The history of the building**
- **The site location**
- **The architectural style of the existing building**
- **The condition of the building**
- **The materials used in construction**

Employing a bold spatial tactic such as the 'space within a space' strategy (see page 50) can be the conceptual driving force for a scheme. While this can be seen as a concept based on a design approach, it will often be dependent on, and a response to, the site in question in order to succeed.

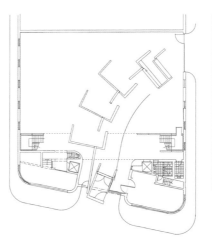
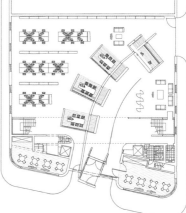

Above
In this student project, the history of a 1930s bus garage is used as a conceptual starting point. Analysis of the building's past uncovered drawings showing the turning circles taken by buses to enter, park in and leave the garage. These arcs were used as a starting point for the spatial organization of a scheme for an advertising agency that was proposed for the space.

Right
Completed in 2008, this project creates offices for an advertising agency in a redundant salt factory. The conceptual idea by Hania Stambuk for the Pullpo Advertising Agency in Santiago, Chile revolves around the approach taken to the introduction of something new to the existing building. The site's derelict condition is preserved and exploited, providing a contrasting context for new elements that are conceived as installations that each act as a 'space within a space'.

Case study Design concepts 1

Cargo, near Geneva, Switzerland / group8

The Swiss architectural firm group8 created Cargo as a studio space for their own practice in 2010. The scheme benefits from a bold and multifaceted conceptual idea.

First, the conceptual idea is concerned with the site in which the interior is to be created. The project is housed in a former industrial building and so a conceptual approach is developed to conceive the space as a storage facility housing large boxes.

Second, a decision is taken to treat shipping containers as 'found objects'. The use of the containers adds a conceptual narrative to the project: the large, colourful metal boxes reference the building's industrial past and also read as volumes that have a temporary relationship with the space within which they are placed. At any time, a container might be sent around the world while another could arrive to replace it.

Third, as a result of the above, the project benefits from a strong conceptual approach to working with an existing building. This might be expected from an architectural practice creating its own workspace but in this instance the strategy of **installation** (see page 118) is implemented in a very assured manner. The host building is refurbished in a simple way and the found shipping containers are placed in the space to great effect. Together they create a stimulating interior where the used shipping containers in random colours are juxtaposed against the clean white building.

Right
The existing architectural envelope has been refurbished in a simple, understated way to create a functional volume. A clean white space is established that clarifies the nature of the industrial architecture and creates an appropriate backdrop for the colourful containers and the creative work of the practice.

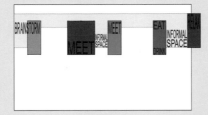

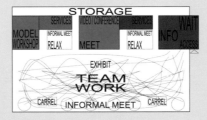

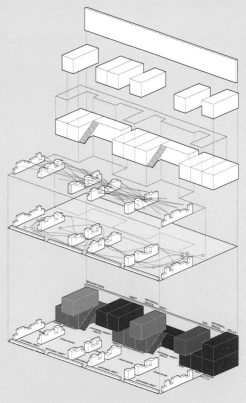

Above
The conceptual diagram for the planning arrangement establishes the idea that the found shipping containers will be 'stored' on top of each other to one side of the warehouse, leaving the rest of the ground floor as studio space. Activities requiring separation or enclosure are allocated to single containers, pairs or triple units as appropriate.

Above
A conceptual isometric drawing shows the containers stacked in the warehouse. On the mezzanine, containers are pulled forward to create a circulation space behind. This solves a practical planning problem while conceptually communicating the notion of a working storage facility where containers are constantly being moved. The random 'found' colours contribute to this idea.

Concepts based on the design approach

The strategy used to create a three-dimensional language is often the main impetus for the development of an interior design scheme. This approach can lead to results where there is a strong contrast between the existing site and the new interior elements that sit within it. The joy of this approach is that it often allows the exploration of fundamental three-dimensional principles such as the use of modular systems or how space can be defined by forming compositions of planes or lines in space. A design approach may investigate 'the temporary' and the implications this might have for the interior specialist working in a more permanent architectural envelope. How are the new elements introduced? What is their lifespan? Will they be reused elsewhere?

Below

This temporary shop was conceived by architects ///byn as a transportable interior that can be installed in sites around the world. The 2011 concept for the Lunar pop-up store in Shanghai, China investigates a design approach that uses a modular system based on triangles, which is then used to create a design language based on three-dimensional nets.

Right

This 2009 scheme by h20 architectes to remodel a child's bedroom in Paris, France uses a design approach that considers the new interior elements as a single piece of bespoke furniture tailor-made for the room it sits within. All the functional requirements are integrated in the new object, which becomes an 'insertion' in the existing space.

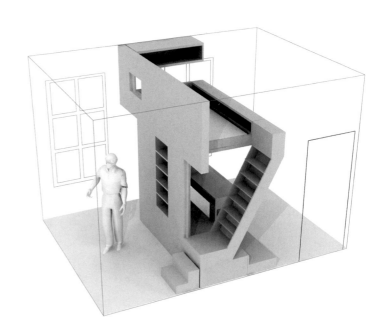

MODULE B

MODULE A

Case study Design concepts 2

Mississippi Blues restaurant, San Francisco, USA / Stanley Saitowitz | Natoma Architects

Mississippi Blues is an unbuilt proposal from 2008 for a soul food restaurant in the Fillmore District of San Francisco, long associated with jazz and blues music. The scheme's planning and three-dimensional form are inspired by a conceptual idea that relates to the restaurant's location and the type of food it serves. The principal design element is the river-like form that meanders through the main dining space. This consists of five separate communal tables above which is a ceiling feature comprising hundreds of hanging brass rods that form a continuous snaking curtain following the plan of the tables. In conceptual terms, the table represents the Mississippi river while the hanging brass rods reference musical instruments used in jazz and blues. True to their conceptual origins, the brass tubes play an acoustical role by acting as a device to deflect sound.

Above
The restaurant's name, Mississippi Blues (a reference to the type of food it would serve), is used as a starting point. Research into the state of Mississippi leads to investigations of the river of the same name, and the form it takes as it meanders through the landscape becomes the key to generating the conceptual idea for the project.

Above
Functional supporting spaces are arranged around two 'closed' sides of the plan to free up the remaining space for the bar and dining area. The conceptual idea is delivered by the central communal table, which takes the form of a river and meanders outside to the pavement, blurring the boundaries between interior and exterior.

Above
In response to the musical references suggested by the restaurant's name and its location in the Historic Fillmore Jazz Preservation District, inspiration is taken from the form and material qualities of brass instruments such as trumpets, saxophones and trombones.

Right
The proposed interior communicates the conceptual idea well, as hundreds of brass rods referencing musical instruments hang above communal dining tables. Together, they act as a river that snakes its way through the space. Lighting levels are kept low to enhance the atmosphere and ensure attention is focused on the brightly lit 'river'.

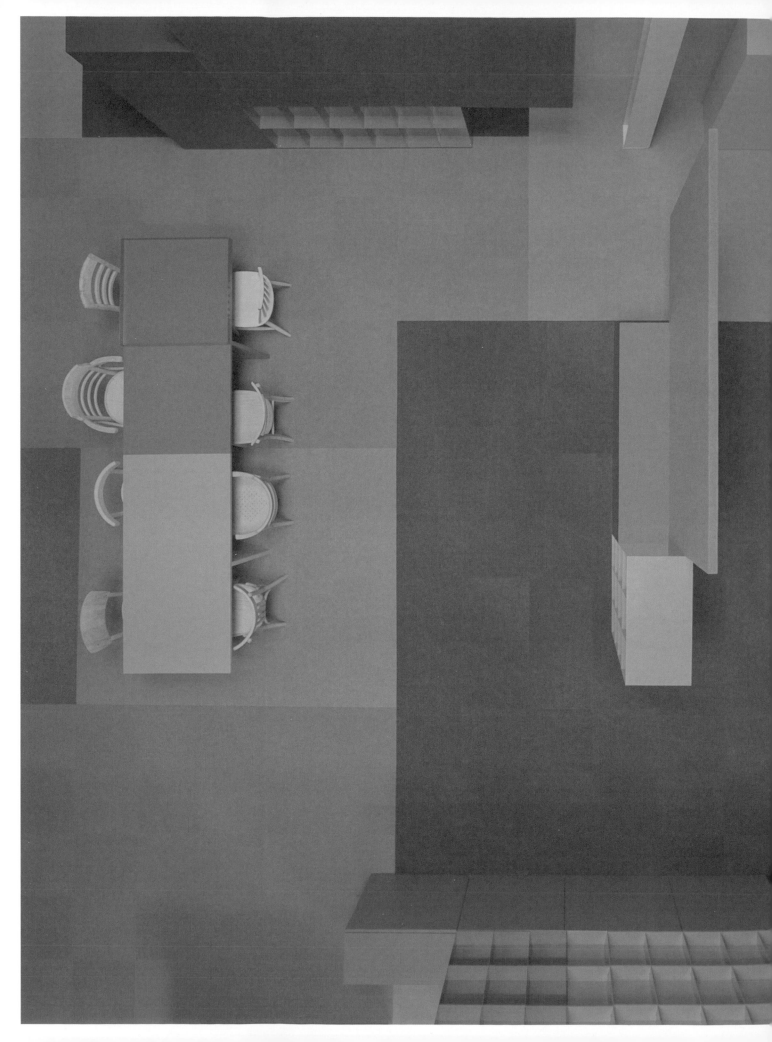

CHAPTER 4
PLANNING STRATEGIES

Introduction

There are a few situations where a building's functional needs might be met by a single space, but the majority of building programmes are far more complex: usually a combination of different spaces is required to create a building that works for its users. Planning strategies are concerned with making decisions about how these spaces should relate to each other and how they should be organized for the building to function as it needs to. Developing a planning strategy for a building involves considering three principal issues that will ultimately be combined to create a diagram that sets out how the building will work.

First, it is important to think about how spaces might relate to one another in terms of their proximity and their separation from each other. This aspect of the work is about spatial relationships. Second, it is important to determine how spaces might be organized in relation to one another so that the building can function as it needs to. A clear policy for the location and organization of an interior's spaces can be described as a spatial strategy. The third consideration is concerned with how spaces are connected to one another and the paths people may choose or be forced to take through a building to access the facilities it provides. This involves determining the interior's circulation strategy. This chapter will examine how these issues can be addressed to create meaningful planning strategies that enable an interior to perform as needed.

Spatial relationships

When two or more distinct spaces are required to enable a building's interior to function, it is inevitable that those spaces will have a relationship with each other. There are four fundamental ways in which two spaces can relate to one another and these can be described in quite simple terms:

- **Space within a space**
- **Overlapping spaces**
- **Adjacent spaces**
- **Spaces linked by a common space**

A **space within a space** occurs when a small space sits within the volume of a larger space, so that it is perceived as an object in that space. The smaller space could be likened to a sculptural object placed in a gallery.

A relationship of **overlapping spaces** is established when two or more spaces are sufficiently defined to ensure that each space has its own identity but can be organized to overlap, so that it might become less obvious where one space stops and the other space starts. The overlapping space might either be perceived as belonging to one of the spaces or as being shared between them.

The most common and straightforward relationship two spaces can have is as **adjacent spaces**. Here the spaces are located next to each other but remain distinct, allowing separate activities to take place in each one.

To create a relationship where **spaces are linked by a common space**, two or more spaces are connected to one another by an additional intermediate space that is shared by all the spaces it serves.

These principles are relatively straightforward but it is crucial for the interior designer to understand them, as how these principles are adapted, developed, combined and utilized is the key to creating interesting, stimulating and sophisticated interior spaces that satisfy the subtle requirements of a building's function.

Space within a space

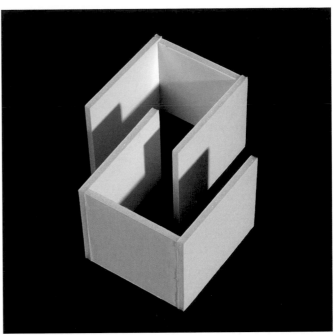

Overlapping spaces

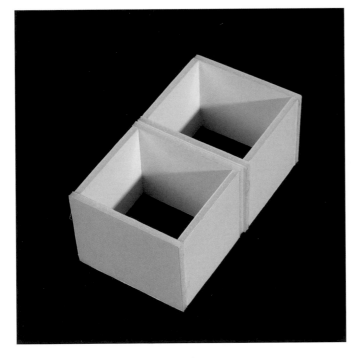

Adjacent spaces

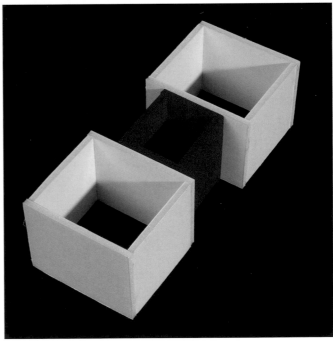

Spaces linked by a common space

Space within a space

The notion of a 'space within a space' provides an interior designer with an exciting opportunity to create quite dramatic compositions in existing buildings. For the strategy to be successful, there needs to be a clear difference in the spatial requirements for the activities contained in the two spaces. The 'host' space must be substantially larger than the space that sits within it, so that the smaller space can be read as an object in the larger volume. For instance, the intimate fitting room spaces in a clothes shop could be placed as stand-alone objects within the larger expanse of the shop floor. Perhaps one of the most famous examples of this strategy in use is Philip Johnson's Glass House, where a cylinder containing the bathroom is placed as an object within the open rectangular floor plan (see pages 28–29).

When using this strategy, the interior designer can manipulate a number of factors to increase the impact of the approach. They might choose to establish a simple relationship between the host space and the space within it by using a similar formal language, colour and materials for both. It may, however, be appropriate to set up a dialogue between the two elements by exploring how the host space might contrast with the smaller space sitting within it, for example through the use of contrasting form, colour, texture and materials in the larger volume. A number of spaces can also exist within a single host space. These smaller spaces could all receive the identical treatment or be treated in similar ways to become a family of related spaces. They could even be individual elements, each one different from the other and the space they sit within. One of the joys of interior design can be working within an existing architectural context: whether the structure is old or new, the particular qualities of the existing building can provide fantastic opportunities for setting up contrasts with the new spaces placed in it.

Below left
In 2001, Coussée & Goris created a centre for the promotion of Flemish produce in the Vleeshuis, a medieval hall in Ghent, Belgium. A modern rectilinear steel and glass box housing a café sits within the stone and timber building fabric, making a clear statement about old and new elements in the scheme.

Below
The Wapping Project, a gallery and restaurant in London, UK occupy a building constructed in 1890 as a hydraulic power station, which closed in the 1970s. As part of the redesign and conversion completed by Shed 54 in 2000, the original building's condition has been preserved; new elements have been placed in it to meet the needs of its new uses. Here a caravan housing a temporary art installation becomes a space within a space.

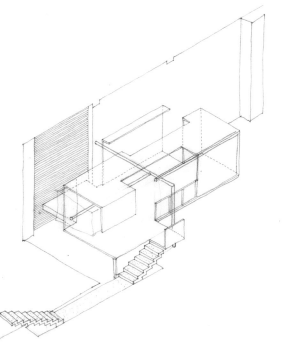

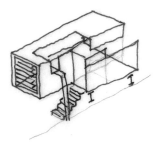

Left

The Innovation Dock is a Dutch education and technology centre housed in the former premises of the Rotterdam Dry Dock Company. The vast existing space has been refurbished and in 2012 a new level containing offices and meeting spaces was constructed in this volume by Groosman Partners. Conceived as a rectilinear object, the new box is perceived as a space within a space.

Left

In this project to create a workspace for Reactor Films in Santa Monica, California the designers Brooks + Scarpa Architects transformed a shipping container into a conference room. Although, as the architects put it, this found object 'has been deconstructed to reveal a richly textured geometry of surfaces and voids', it is essentially an existing space that has been deposited inside a larger volume to create a fantastic example of a space within a space.

Overlapping spaces

For many interior situations, it is important for spaces to be more loosely defined, so that they overlap or flow into each other. The identity of each space involved in the composition can be more or less dominant, and space can be shared by a number of zones. The form and positioning of floors, walls and ceilings can allow spaces to be defined as separate and combined as necessary. For instance, three spaces may form an overlapping relationship where one space is defined by a base plane (floor), another by a vertical plane (wall) and the third by an overhead plane (ceiling).

In the late nineteenth century, Frank Lloyd Wright began exploring the concept that spaces could overlap, and his ideas emerged in the house he built for his family in Oak Park, Illinois in 1889. In a series of studies and buildings dating from the 1920s, Mies van der Rohe developed ways in which interior spaces could cease to be separate cellular entities and begin to flow into one another. His proposal for a Brick Country House (1923) introduced a composition of free-standing brick walls that were arranged to create a series of overlapping and interconnecting spaces. The Villa Tugendhat (Brno, Czechoslovakia, 1928–30) and the Barcelona Pavilion (1929) delivered overlapping spaces in a built form for the first time and revolutionized the way in which internal spaces could be planned and used.

Below
Canadian practice RUF Project designed the Nike Football Training Centre in Soweto, South Africa. Completed in 2010, the scheme features interior spaces in which finishes and materials are layered to create a collage of overlapping spaces that are at once dynamic and informal.

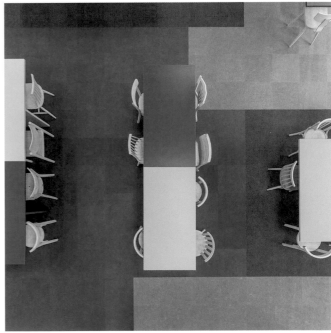

This page

Combiwerk Delft, completed in 2012, is a 'social workplace' company that helps people with physical or mental problems back into employment. Dutch design practice i29 created a grey envelope that is then occupied by islands of bold colours. Within each zone identified by a single colour, the spaces overlap and interlock, softening the boundaries between different activities taking place within the same space. Layers of various tones of the same hue are carefully used to enhance this spatial strategy.

Adjacent spaces

Adjacent spaces are the most common form of spatial relationship. While the idea of creating a series of fluid, interconnected and overlapping spaces is seductive, in many circumstances it is necessary to create a collection of spaces that are separated by physical divisions, allowing each space to have its own identity and host the required activity. Adjacent spaces might be completely divorced from each other (located next to each other on plan but the user cannot transfer from one space to the other) or they may have a very open relationship – two adjacent spaces could be defined as being different by a simple line drawn on the floor, like the two halves of a football pitch.

As adjacent spaces can be established by complete physical division at one extreme through to a barely defined delineation of the spaces involved at the other, the interior designer is presented with countless opportunities between these approaches. Indeed a key aspect of the interior designer's work involves considering how adjacent spaces can be defined in ways that are neither black nor white, neither completely open nor completely closed. The grey area in between provides the opportunity for spaces to be distinguished from each other in interesting ways.

Below

The galleries of the Sainsbury Wing, an extension of the National Gallery in London, UK are accessed either via a grand staircase or lifts (elevators) from the new ground-floor entrance foyer or by a link bridge from the existing building. The new second-floor galleries are made up of 16 separate rooms arranged in three adjacent rows. Within these rows, rooms have an adjacent relationship with each other. Architects Venturi, Scott Brown and Associates considered this traditional arrangement of spaces to be an appropriate response to the world-class collection of early Renaissance art the new galleries would house.

Right

Opened in 1991, the building features gallery spaces conceived as clearly defined rooms that enjoy adjacent spatial relationships. A view through the central galleries shows four adjacent spaces, each defined as a separate room that allows small-scale paintings to be viewed in intimate surroundings, while the arched openings arranged around a central axis make it possible to view large-scale works from an appropriate distance.

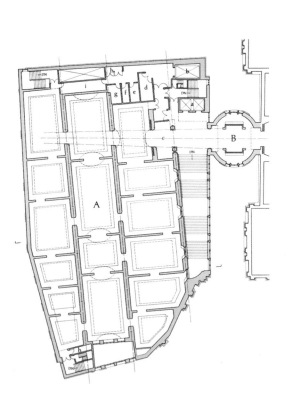

Spaces linked by a common space

A number of spaces can be arranged so that they are separated from each other but connected by an additional common space. This spatial relationship can enable related spaces to retain their individual autonomy while retaining their connection to a single entity. Shared by the separate spaces, the common space acts as a transitional zone from one space to another, providing the user with a choice as to which spaces they enter and in what order they encounter them. Typical examples of this kind of arrangement include a multiplex cinema where a number of separate screens are connected by a large vestibule; a

museum where a series of exhibition spaces are arranged around a communal space; or a school building where classrooms are organized around a common social zone.

Depending on the activities taking place in them, the spaces being linked may be larger or smaller than the common space they share, they may all be the same size or different sizes, and they may be organized in a formal or informal manner. The opportunities offered by the existing site and the precise nature of the building programme will determine these decisions.

Left
Completed in 2000, Foster + Partners' scheme for the Great Court at the British Museum in London transformed a neglected exterior space into a magnificent light-filled interior space that has become the 'hub' of the museum.

Below
A new glass and steel roof structure creates an internal courtyard that establishes the common space linking the central cylindrical reading room of the old British Library with the museum's entrance and the gallery spaces arranged around the four sides of the square courtyard.

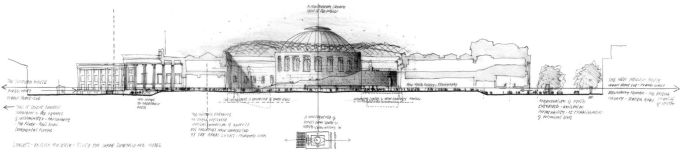

Right
Prior to the redevelopment, the courtyard was used as an impromptu storage area and closed to the public. As the existing galleries were arranged around the courtyard, they became a series of adjacent spaces organized in a linear configuration that had become confused over the years. The under-utilized space between the galleries and the cylindrical reading room provided an opportunity to reinvent the museum.

Far right
A previously redundant lost space has become a spectacular light-infused volume enjoyed by visitors all year round. The new common space plays host to a number of visitor facilities, including information points and temporary exhibitions as well as shops, cafés and restaurants. The Great Court also provides users with a clear reference point that helps them make sense of the gallery spaces it links together.

Spatial strategies

When planning a building's interior, the fundamental ways in which spaces are related to each other are perhaps the first aspect that must be understood, but, arguably, the second issue for the designer to consider is the strategy they will employ to organize the spaces. There are five discrete strategies the interior designer can use to organize spaces:

- **Linear strategies**
- **Grid strategies**
- **Radial strategies**
- **Centralized strategies**
- **Clustered strategies**

A **linear strategy** involves arranging a number of different spaces in a line. The spaces might be identical or they might all be different.

When using a **grid strategy**, a collection of spaces is organized around a formal network of lines (usually set out on a rectilinear x–y axis). This may be a two-dimensional (plan) strategy or a three-dimensional (volumetric) strategy. In a three-dimensional arrangement of spaces, the network of lines used to formalize the configuration will include x, y and z axes. This approach will often involve the arrangement of a number of identically sized rectilinear spaces, or it will operate around a module size, where all the individual spaces are related to the size of the organizing grid (for example by incorporating 'double' or 'triple' unit spaces).

A **radial strategy** is created when a number of spaces journey outwards from a space of origin. The radial spaces may form a symmetrical or asymmetrical relationship with the space of origin, and they may be identical or different from each other.

A **centralized strategy** occurs when a single space occupies the middle of a configuration and a number of other spaces are organized around it. The surrounding spaces might all be the same or they might be completely different.

A number of identical or different spaces can be combined in an informal way through the use of a **clustered strategy**. Here the size and shape of the individual spaces might vary, and they could be organized in asymmetrical configurations in which spaces overlap.

In reality, most interior design problems are far too complex for a single spatial strategy to be the answer to the programme's needs and the successful planning solution may employ all the tactics described above.

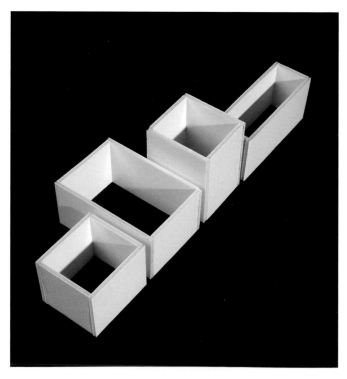

A linear strategy

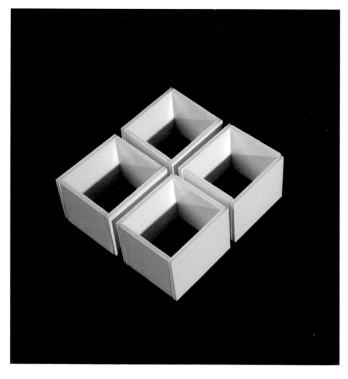

A grid strategy

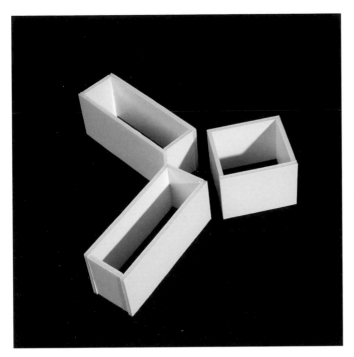

A radial strategy

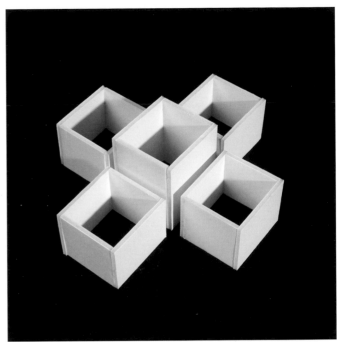

A centralized strategy

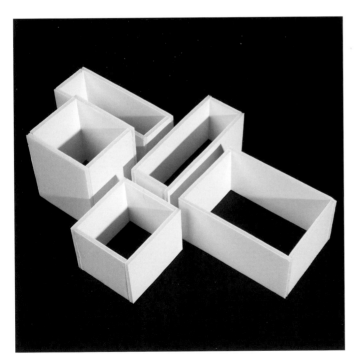

A clustered strategy

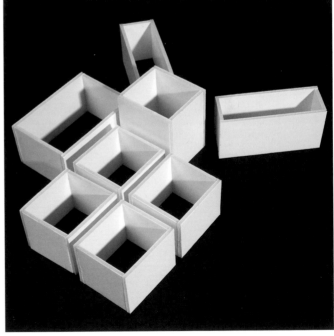

The spatial strategy for a single interior scheme
might employ all these approaches.

STEP BY STEP DRAWING DIAGRAMS

Designers use diagrams as a means of communicating complex ideas in simpler terms. Diagrams are an important part of the design process, enabling the interior designer to explore a spatial problem and quickly identify a number of possible solutions. As well as being an integral part of a scheme's design development, diagrams are important tools when it comes to communicating proposals to colleagues and clients. Diagrams should clarify and simplify to ensure that the crucial aspects of the proposal are understood. They are often used to discuss ideas and approaches during the early stages of a project, when many routes towards a satisfactory solution remain available. Because the proposals are still open and unresolved, it is often useful to communicate the content using freehand drawings, as they are more forgiving and less 'final' than computer-generated material.

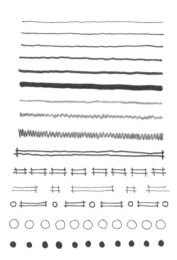

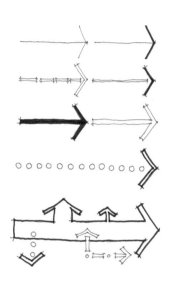

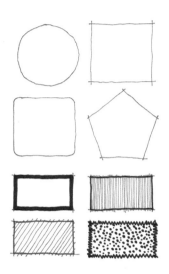

1 **Lines**: different quality of line forms the basis of a good diagram. A variety of line weights can be achieved by using pens of different thicknesses, and this helps diagrams to read more clearly. A range of line types such as outlines, dashed lines, chain lines and dotted lines are also useful when trying to communicate difference.

2 **Arrows**: a range of arrow types can be utilized to establish different types of connections in a diagram. The weight of arrows can relate to the importance of connections and the size of arrows might provide information about the flow of people on major and minor routes.

3 **Shapes**: simple primary shapes allow a diagram to communicate clearly. Different spaces may be 'coded' by the use of different shapes or the same shape may be used in a variety of sizes to communicate hierarchy. Line weights can further emphasize particular shapes and hatching can identify difference.

ABCDEFGHIJK

ABCDEFGHIJK

ABCDEFGHIJK

ABCDEFGHIJK

ABCDEFGHIJK

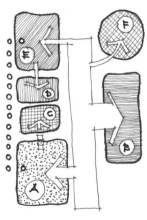

4 **Words**: most diagrams need to include words to aid understanding. It helps if the designer's handwriting is confident and legible, otherwise text can be traced or even added digitally once the hand-drawn diagram has been scanned.

5 **Underlay sheets**: diagrams can be produced quickly and with confidence by tracing from an underlay sheet. A variety of useful diagram elements such as shapes, lines, arrows and text can be printed from a computer and then used to construct hand-drawn diagrams. An underlay sheet printed on to brightly coloured card will be easy to find on the designer's desk.

6 **Finished Diagrams**: a successful diagram will often incorporate different qualities of line, arrows, shapes and hatching as well as text.

Linear strategies

Perhaps the most straightforward way in which to organize spaces is a linear arrangement. This solution is appropriate for use in situations where clarity, simplicity and ease of navigation are required. An additional consideration may be concerned with economy – a linear plan can provide an effective solution when resources are limited (this might be a matter of space, budget or both). Interior typologies where a linear strategy is commonly employed include cellular office environments, shopping centres, educational buildings, the residential areas of hotels and even transport interiors such as train carriages and passenger aeroplanes.

Although a linear relationship implies a series of spaces positioned in a straight line, this is not necessarily the case: a number of spaces could, for example, be placed in a linear sequence that forms a circular plan. When it comes to the form the interior designer's planning proposal will take, the opportunities available are invariably driven by the constraints of the building in which the interior is to be housed.

Below
Completed in 2010 by Bates Smart Architects, the Crown Metropol Hotel in Melbourne, Australia features 658 guest rooms arranged over 18 floors. On each floor, the accommodation is organized according to a linear spatial strategy. A central corridor runs the length of the building, connecting rooms and vertical circulation while simultaneously separating bedrooms located to either side. The prospect of a relentless corridor is alleviated by the sinuous curving plan, which shows how a simple linear arrangement can create a dynamic solution.

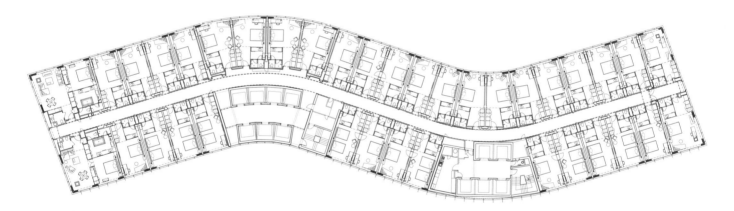

Left
Due to the form of the aircraft, the interior of a passenger jet inevitably utilizes a linear planning solution. In Virgin Atlantic's new Upper Class suite, created in 2012 by Virgin Atlantic's in-house design team in collaboration with Pengelly Design, seats are arranged in an angled linear configuration to maximize density while optimizing comfort.

Grid strategies

As grid strategies are often employed by architects to design the buildings the interior specialist works within, they can be an effective way of utilizing the opportunities presented by a host structure. Like a linear strategy, the grid strategy can be highly efficient, allowing functional spaces to be created with relative ease.

Of course, in the contemporary world the grid can be seen as dehumanizing and indeed a grid organization is often implemented in situations where a sense of order and control is appropriate – this may be in a more formal workplace such as a call centre, in a factory or a prison. In a library or a supermarket, a grid strategy may be the perfect method of bringing order and clarity to the vast amount of material the interior's users need to navigate and access, with the grid layout acting as coordinates that allow them to reach precise locations quickly and easily.

A grid strategy can also be used to contradict the grain of an existing building. This might involve using the dimensions of the building's existing grid to inform the dimensions of the grid used to define new interior spaces, but then placing this new grid in a contrary orientation to set up a dialogue between the existing building and the new interior. A completely alien grid could be introduced to order new interior elements within an existing space, again offering an opportunity to explore the potential for contrast.

Above
In Jacques Tati's 1967 film *Playtime*, the main character, Monsieur Hulot, is confronted by a series of inhumane Modernist scenarios, including this workplace where employees are isolated in identical cubicles organized on a repetitive grid.

Right
At the Cultural Centre in Zlín, the Czech Republic, Eva Jiricna Architects used a straightforward grid to organize the fixed seating in the lozenge-shaped auditorium space. This project was completed in 2011.

Left
In the ANA Lounge at Ota-ku airport, Tokyo, Japan completed in 2011 by Nikken Space Design, a ceiling grid is used to organize the seating areas below it.

Radial strategies

While there are many building programmes that will not be able to utilize a radial strategy, there are also plenty of situations in which a radial strategy is the only possible solution.

A radial planning solution can have as few as two or a huge number of 'spokes' making their journey away from the initial common space. Each arm might be identical and house exactly the same facilities (such as in an airport, where a series of boarding gates radiate from the airside departure lounge) or each arm could be different in size, form and function (such as in a school, where different arms contain the library, the refectory, the sports facilities and the classrooms).

The initial communal space can act as a 'hub' that serves as a crucial support for the activities located in the various 'spokes' radiating out from the centre. For instance, in a hotel the bedrooms could be located in the spokes and the hospitality facilities in the central space.

While it may not be possible for the interior designer working with an existing building to employ a radial planning strategy due to the restrictions of the existing site, it is, however, crucial for them to be aware of the constraints and opportunities that this plan type presents, so that when they are faced with a site that has been organized around a radial strategy, they will know how to take advantage of the situation.

Below
Ron Herron's 1987 sketch describes a proposed studio for the multidisciplinary creative company Imagination. The plan revolves around a central communal 'hub' space, from which different team spaces radiate. This sketch diagram/plan explains a big idea in a lively manner.

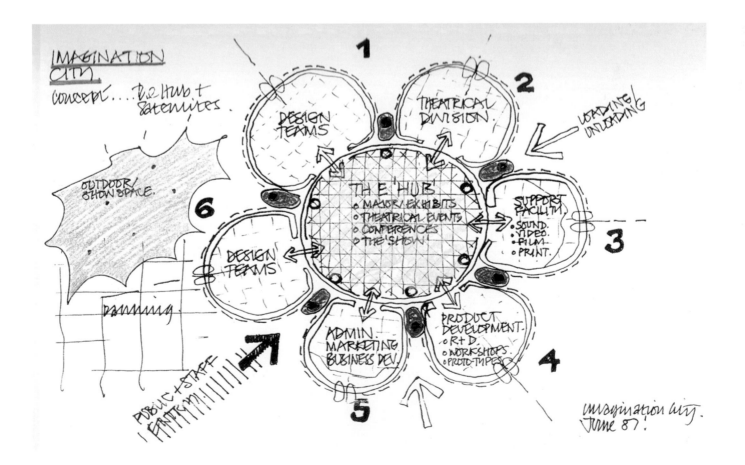

Centralized strategies

Although there are some similarities between radial and centralized planning configurations, there are also fundamental differences. While a radial plan is essentially an outward-facing solution, where the building journeys outwards in a number of directions from a central point of origin, a centralized plan is fundamentally an introverted arrangement, with a collection of smaller spaces organized around a central space that is the dominant space in the composition. This central space is often a bold geometrical shape, such as square, circular or octagonal. Although the secondary spaces surrounding the dominant central space can all assume different forms, a centralized strategy is often used in situations where a clear sense of order is required to enable users to understand the activities within the space. As a result, the larger dominant central space is often surrounded by a number of identical secondary spaces whose forms can be sympathetic to, or contrast with, each other.

The centralized plan is perhaps most commonly associated with Italian churches of the Renaissance period, but is utilized today in large communal spaces that need to be serviced by a number of different activities. One example would be a food court in a shopping centre: the communal dining area is the central space, which is surrounded by secondary spaces that offer a variety of different food outlets, each housed in an identical subservient space.

Left
Designed by Andrea Palladio, the Villa Rotonda was completed near Vicenza, Italy in 1570. This study by Oliver Lam-Watson, Kingston University, UK shows the circular space centralized within the square building plan.

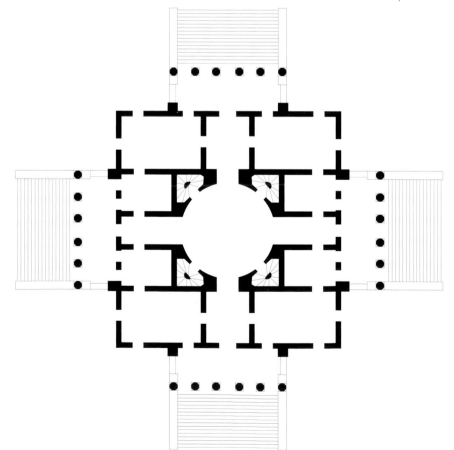

Clustered strategies

A clustered organization can be an appropriate response when a sense of informality is required. This approach can be equally successful whether the spaces to be arranged are identical or different. When there is a need for identical spaces, the clustered arrangement can soften the repetitive patterns a more formal spatial arrangement might establish, while spaces of different sizes and shapes can be arranged to form relaxed relationships, because there are no rigid, geometrical rules to adhere to in terms of the layout. A clustered strategy can also work well when dealing with different spatial relationships, such as overlapping or adjacent spaces. Thanks to its informality, it is easy to amend through addition or subtraction – it is an essentially 'open' system that is neither finished nor unfinished.

Interior designers often use clustered strategies when planning spatial arrangements for leisure and hospitality spaces such as restaurants, bars and nightclubs, where the aim is to create a relaxed environment. In some retail situations, such as department stores, this approach can succeed by enticing customers into different zones, while museum and exhibition designers employ clustered strategies to encourage visitors to explore displays. As the clustered plan can encourage human interaction, it is frequently used in the organization of spatial strategies for creative workplaces.

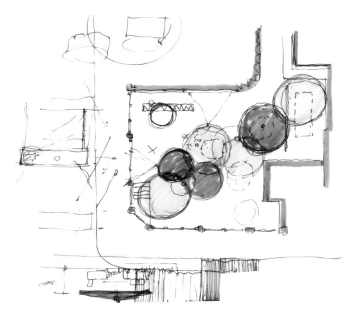

Above
The Steelcase Worklife showroom in London, UK by Pearson Lloyd Design Studio Ltd (2007), features a plan configured from a collection of circular spaces of various sizes that are layered on top of each other to form a clustered plan.

Below
Curiosity, a design practice based in Japan, created this proposal for the urban Meilo Hotel in 2007. The scheme features an atrium space defined by suspended cubic spaces that are arranged in a clustered formation.

Circulation strategies

In terms of interior design, circulation involves the ways in which users navigate the spaces within a building. As most buildings consist of more than a single space, the circulation strategy is concerned with the order in which users experience the spaces provided. A circulation strategy will determine when users should be compelled to enter a space, be given the option of entering a space or perhaps be prohibited from entering some spaces while being allowed access to others.

In some interiors, each user takes the same route (an exhibition with a prescribed pathway from start to finish, for example), but even in these situations the circulation may be more complex (the visitors to the exhibition may all be following the same circulation route while the staff are using a different one). In most buildings, users take their own route through the spaces provided in response to the restrictions placed on them, which makes it possible for each visitor to circulate around the building in a different way. However complex the circulation strategy of a building may become, one thing remains simple: as people circulate through buildings they take a path and by its nature this path is a linear route that takes the user on a journey through time and space. It is this principle that underpins the formation of circulation strategies that enable people to navigate buildings as required. The linear route can be organized as:

• **A radial circulation**
• **A spiral circulation**
• **A grid circulation**
• **A network circulation**

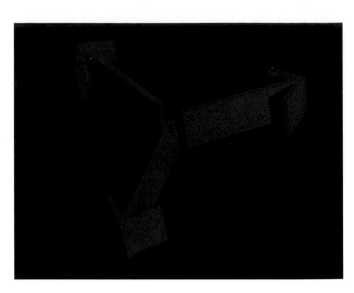

A radial circulation strategy

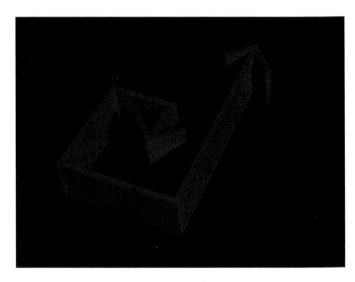

A spiral circulation strategy

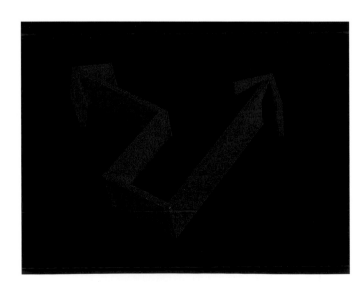

All circulation is a linear activity.

When a number of paths converge at a single point, a **radial circulation** strategy is established. A **spiral circulation** strategy begins (or ends) in the middle and rotates outwards around the point of origin. If paths are configured as sets of parallel lines that intersect with one another to define rectilinear spaces, then a **grid circulation** strategy is formed. When very specific points in an interior's plan are connected by a number of paths that otherwise appear quite arbitrary, then a **network circulation** strategy is employed.

It is important to remember that an interior's spatial and circulation strategies are different things, and that the juxtaposition of these two components determines how the building works. For instance, an interior's spaces might have a **centralized** organization accessed by a **grid circulation** strategy.

A grid circulation strategy

A network circulation strategy

While the interior designer is primarily concerned with circulation within the building, in many situations it is impossible to divorce the interior from the exterior. The location of a building's entrance is often appropriate, well established or impossible to move, and as a result it can be a major factor in determining how the building is planned. In other instances, the entrance(s) to the building can be repositioned, which the designer might choose to do in order to improve the relationship of the entrance to the interior's plan, to the approach to the building or to both. Whatever the context for subsequent decisions, a building's circulation strategy has three distinct phases that the interior designer should consider:

- **The approach**
- **The entrance**
- **The path**

Paths

For interior designers, a path is the course people take in and around buildings. Interior spaces can either control the way in which people circulate – the corridor that prescribes a route, for example – or be quite open, allowing users to navigate the spaces in any way they wish. Different functional needs will require different circulation solutions. However, whether prescribed or not, all paths through buildings are, by their very nature, linear and involve a journey through time and space. Some interior solutions will demand efficiency and the creation of paths that connect spaces as quickly as possible (perhaps in a workplace) while in other situations it may be appropriate to force the user to journey along a prolonged pathway through the interior (perhaps in an exhibition where information is disseminated along the route).

When working in an existing building, the interior designer's aim may be to establish restricted circulation through the structure's large open spaces or to create greater freedom of circulation between a series of cellular spaces that currently constrain ease of movement.

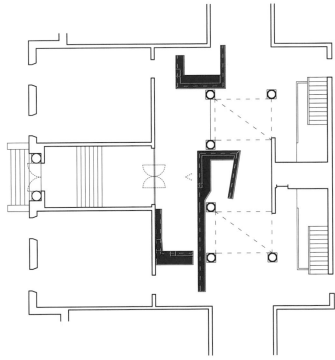

Above

In their 2009 conversion of a former maternity hospital, RaichdelRio introduced three furniture elements to reconfigure the circulation route of the entrance to offices for the Catalan health service in Barcelona, Spain. The first two objects form a barrier that divides the public area from the secure side of the foyer, providing desks for reception and security staff. Visitors are obliged to circulate between the two desks, where security turnstiles limit access. Beyond the secure line, the third element of the composition provides seating in a waiting area. Together, the elements restrict physical access but allow the whole space to remain visible.

The approach

The user's first encounter with a building occurs in the approach. The approach may involve a long sequence of events where, for example, the user first sees the building while driving past and then subsequently approaches it on foot, having parked the car, or it can be an instantaneous event, with the building being one of many with similar facades relating to a street and approached along the pavement. Obviously, the approach has a direct relationship with the building's entrance: it can terminate there or continue through the entrance to become the interior's circulation route.

While an architect may design the building and the approach to it, the interior designer will generally be working within an existing context, where the approach is already established. The interior designer needs to understand the issues involved in the approach to an existing building in order to be able to respond as necessary. For example, the designer could be working with a building that was designed to respond to the site conditions at the time of construction but, due to subsequent changes to the local environment, the approach/entrance sequence is no longer appropriate. Alternatively, the demands of a new interior may mean that a new approach is needed for the redeveloped building to operate successfully. When situations such as these occur, the interior designer may need to establish a new approach or consider how the existing approach can be made to work better. It is therefore important to understand the ways in which a building can be approached:

- **Frontal approach**
- **Oblique approach**
- **Spiral approach**

Above
Oblique approach: completed in 1993, the Storefront for Art and Architecture in New York, NY, USA was designed by artist Vito Acconci and architect Steven Holl. The gallery occupies a long, thin, wedge-shaped space in lower Manhattan and is approached along the pavement, with the path being parallel to the building's envelope. The facade consists of 12 pivoting panels that open up to invite passers-by into the space – a device that blurs the boundaries between inside and outside and responds to the direction of approach.

Top right
Frontal approach: Broadway Malyan's 2008 refurbishment of the Rossio railway station in Lisbon, Portugal restored the facade of the 1887 building. The symmetrical elevation with the clearly identified centralized entrance point is an ideal response to the main pedestrian access to the building, which is established by the location of the pedestrian crossing.

Right and below right
Spiral approach: the approach to the Drents Archive at Assens in the Netherlands provides visitors with a view of the white cube added by Zecc Architects as part of a major renovation in 2012, but a pathway takes them on a route through the gardens and around the existing building before finally delivering them at the front of the new entrance pavilion.

Entrance

The approach to a building will eventually lead to the entrance and, although building entrances can be defined in a multitude of ways, they will inevitably fall into one of three categories. The relationship of the approach to the point of entry and the form of the building will inform the decision as to which of the following entrance types is appropriate in a particular instance:

- **Flush entrance**
- **Projected entrance**
- **Recessed entrance**

When dealing with an existing building, the interior designer may face restrictions as to what they can do to change the established form of the entrance, or there may be an opportunity to modify the entrance within the existing aperture to create a new statement of entry that signifies to the outside world that the interior has been changed. In cases where a new point of entrance is established in the fabric of an existing building, the designer will have much more freedom to create a proposal that is appropriate for the new interior while responding to the demands of the approach and the building envelope. This strategy provides the designer with exciting opportunities to juxtapose old and new building elements, emphasizing the notion that a site has undergone some form of change.

Right
Flush entrance: when this house in London, UK was subdivided into apartments in 2004, a new entrance was required. The restrictions of the site made it impossible for the entrance to project or be recessed, so Groves Natcheva Architects designed a square panel of black metal that floats on the existing brick wall. This signifies that the interior of the building has been altered, while the apertures within the panel suggest a point of entrance.

Above
Projected entrance: completed in 2002, another residential project by Groves Natcheva Architects called for a different solution. Here a four-storey terraced house in south-east London, UK was converted into flats and access to a new first-floor entrance to the rear of the property was required. A metal staircase is housed within a folded metal plane that projects out of the building into the rear yard, inviting visitors to enter.

Left
Recessed entrance: for a Commes des Garçons shop in Tokyo, Japan completed in 1998, Future Systems removed the existing glass shopfront at the ground floor of a rather ordinary office building and created a new sloping, curved glass facade that draws customers into an entrance that is recessed into the shop itself.

Case Study Entrance

Art Gallery, Vienna, Austria / Adolf Krischanitz

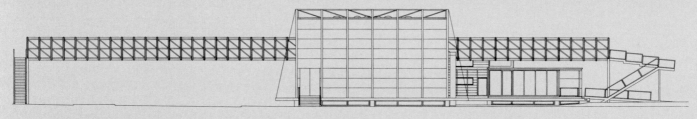

Completed in 1994, this temporary art gallery was located on a traffic island in Vienna's city centre. In terms of physical access alone, the location presented a challenge. And how might passers-by be presented with some clues that this closed yellow box, isolated from its immediate environment by the surrounding main road, could be entered at all? The clever planning solution turns the entrance sequence into a journey made up of a series of events that blur the boundaries between inside and outside.

The solution revolves around the gallery being conceived as a box with its back turned to the surrounding road: a cylindrical tube piercing the building's rectilinear form becomes a bridge over the road on one side of the box and a means of delivering visitors to the entrance on the other side. The entrance is located on the island, in a space protected from the surrounding traffic by the building itself. The user may be unclear as to whether they are inside or outside or the building, which side is the 'front' and which the 'back' and exactly where they entered it. All these uncertainties seem appropriate for a space designed to house contemporary art.

Top
A pair of staircases address both directions of approach along the pavement and take visitors up to the elevated cylindrical walkway, which acts as a bridge across the road. Although undoubtedly still an external space, the steel cage structure creates some enclosure and begins to blur the boundaries between exterior and interior. The walkway enters the main volume of the building at a high level.

Below
Once the road has been traversed, the walkway penetrates the gallery space volume. At this point, it becomes an opaque tube, obscuring views of the artwork, and the journey continues out the other side of the box. Visitors are left uncertain as to whether they have been inside the building or not.

Above
The side elevation and plan show how the gallery is situated on the traffic island and that the entrance sequence begins on the other side of the road. The cylindrical raised walkway (accessed by staircases) acts as a bridge across the main road before penetrating the main exhibition hall and then exiting it on the opposite side. The journey proceeds to a staircase that turns the circulation through 180 degrees, depositing visitors at the doors leading to the gallery's initial interior spaces.

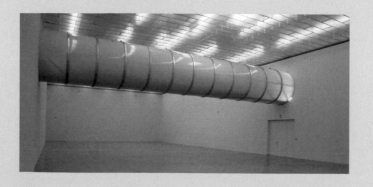

Circulation and space

For the interior designer, a crucial aspect of the planning process is establishing the relationship between the paths people take through a building and the spaces allocated for specific functions. An interior's circulation routes and its spaces must have a relationship of some kind and there are only three options:

- **Pass-through-space circulation**
- **Pass-by-space circulation**
- **Terminate-in-a-space circulation**

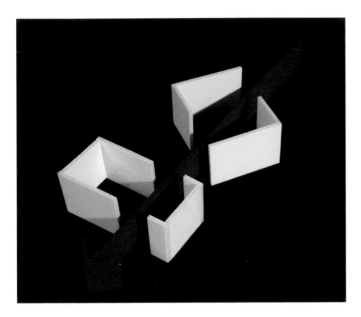

A pass-through-space circulation

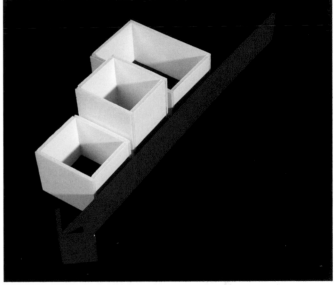

A pass-by-space circulation

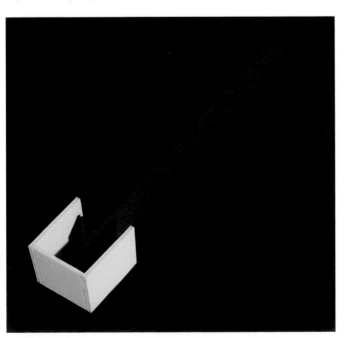

A terminate-in-a-space circulation

Pass-through-space circulation

If a path takes the user through an interior space that houses other activities, then this may be termed a pass-through-space circulation type. The path can take users to one side of the space, through the middle or on a circuitous route through it, thus providing the interior designer with an opportunity to configure the circulation route to help define the activity zones within the space. This strategy can be applied to many situations – in a department store, for example, where the primary circulation path might meander around a given floor, defining spaces that house particular departments or concessions.

Depending on the requirements of the programme, the interior designer will decide whether a direct or indirect path is appropriate, and whether users may be free to leave the path at any time or be constrained to it – allowed to view the space the circulation passes through but without being granted physical access.

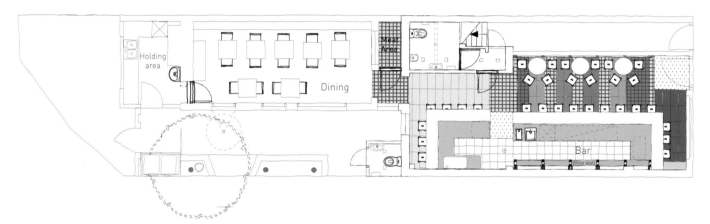

Above
This sketch plan shows how Phi Design & Architecture's 2011 scheme for the Wine Library bar and restaurant in Woollahra, Australia resolves the challenges of a tight existing building by turning the main bar area into a pass-through-space circulation route that provides access to toilets, the service area and the dining space located at the rear of the site.

Right
View showing the pass-through-space circulation route established between the servery and the seating area of the Wine Library's bar area. Customers are free to proceed along the route, visit the servery or sit at the tables.

Right and far right
The offices of advertising and design agency KMS Team in Munich, Germany, completed in 2000, are housed in a former industrial building, where an existing bridge provided an opportunity for a high-level circulation route to be established. The bridge connects the reception area to meeting rooms located at the rear of the building and passes through the main studio space, offering clients views of activity in the workspaces below.

Pass-by-space circulation

There are many interior situations where it would be inappropriate for the general circulation path to proceed through a given space. Often particular spaces require privacy – hotel bedrooms and doctors' consulting rooms, for example – while access must be provided to other spaces in the building. In circumstances such as these, a pass-by-space circulation strategy can be employed. The journey that passes by a given space may be contained within a specific path designated only for circulation (a corridor), or a route could pass through a space containing some public activities while at the same time passing by private spaces located within or adjacent to the primary space. Typically, this scenario might be established in a workplace, where an open-plan office may contain a pass-through-space circulation route that also passes by cellular offices and adjacent meeting rooms.

A pass-by-space circulation strategy provides the interior's users with a choice as to which spaces are accessed and the order in which this access is granted.

Right
Completed in 2010, Adolf Krischanitz's Archive of Contemporary Arts in Krems, Austria groups together four reading rooms to form a rectangular box that reads as a space within a space. A corridor surrounds this block, providing a pass-by-space circulation path that allows visitors to access any of the rooms in any order, as well as ensuring that activities taking place in any given room can continue uninterrupted.

Below
A view showing the corridor that provides a pass-by-space circulation around the rectangular box housing the four reading rooms.

Bottom right
Activity in the reading rooms can remain uninterrupted thanks to the pass-by-space circulation strategy used to access them.

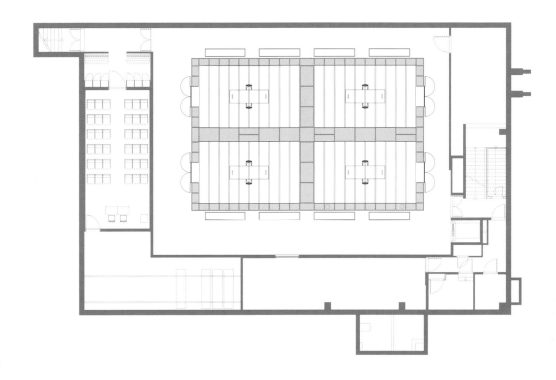

Terminate-in-a-space circulation

While some spaces enable users to proceed further into the building, there are many interior situations where a given space is the end of a circulation path. As a consequence, the visitor must exit via the point of entrance, retracing their steps in order to leave the space. When this situation arises, circulation terminates in the given space. This is a common situation that occurs many times over in most buildings: cellular offices, restrooms and storage rooms are all spaces where a termination of the circulation path will occur.

The space in which the circulation terminates may be a support space of minor importance in the building or it could be a very special space, which celebrates the culmination of the journey taken to reach it. Often, drama can be created by establishing contrasts between the circulation path and the space in which it terminates: for example, a dark, confined route can arrive at a huge, light-filled volume.

Above
Each fitting room cubicle in Left, a fashion boutique in Melbourne, Australia designed in 2007 by Russell & George, is a space that terminates the circulation route, making it necessary for users to retrace their steps in order to exit.

Right
Russell & George created this small retail unit for Aesop in Doncaster, Australia in 2008. The scheme consists of a single space that becomes a termination of the circulation path taken to reach it.

Above
A cellular office, such as this example in the Justice Precinct Office in Sydney, Australia, completed in 2007 by Bates Smart Architects, will provide a space that terminates the circulation path in a workplace.

Below left and right
Completed in 2013, the Silence Room designed by Alex Cochrane Architects at Selfridges department store in London, UK takes visitors on a journey along a dark circulation path that terminates in a soft, calm, light-filled space.

Planning solutions

On rare occasions, the demands of a building programme can be met by one bold, simple planning strategy, but most interior situations require a spatial solution that is much more sophisticated. The majority of finished interior schemes are likely to incorporate a response to some or all of the following issues:

- **Approach**
- **Entrance**
- **Spatial strategy**
- **Spatial relationships**
- **Circulation strategy**

In order for a building to function correctly, a single interior might be configured using a complex collection of spatial relationships and include a number of different circulation strategies. While it is possible to isolate and separate approaches to the above issues, solutions are often complex and ambiguous (for example, a plan might be organized in a linear way that is also a grid organization), providing sophisticated, nuanced arrangements to satisfy a set of complex human requirements. All this becomes much more complex when the interior designer is operating within an existing building that presents its own constraints: the functional requirements of a particular programme may be resolved by a planning diagram that works in principle but cannot be imposed on the site without some compromise. As a result, the interior designer is often concerned with reconciling the ideal of the perfect diagram with the reality of the existing interior spaces and their inherent restrictions.

Right
In 2007 Ippolito Fleitz Group created this radiology clinic in Schorndorf, Germany. The design provides a spatial solution for a demanding brief: the interior must meet a highly technical functional specification while providing a comforting environment for patients. A controlled reception zone leads on to the centralized waiting area around which the main circulation path is wrapped. The consulting rooms are arranged in a linear configuration to one side of the plan, while the treatment spaces are organized in a linear, then clustered, arrangement around the remaining two lengths of corridor.

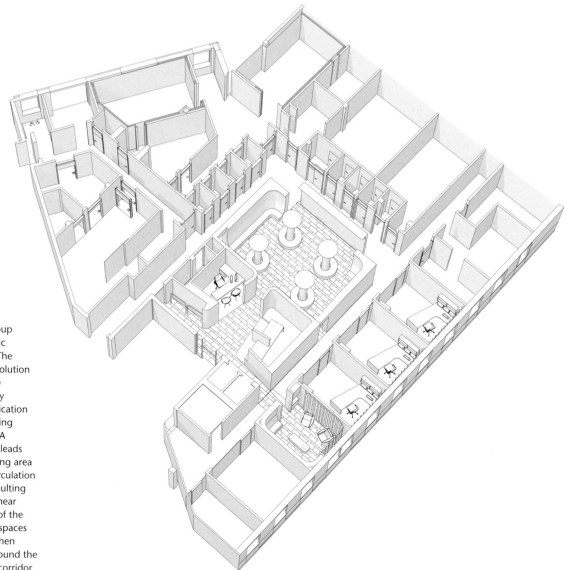

Right
The pass-through-space entrance area establishes a clear route to the waiting area for visitors while ensuring security and staff supervision.

Below
The waiting area is centralized within the building, enabling it to act as the secure 'heart' of the space, from which patients can access other facilities. Seating is organized in a radial configuration around the columns, which helps to create more informal groupings of people.

Left and above
Organized in a linear manner, the consulting rooms respond simply to the building's structural grid and are terminate spaces.

Far left
A single pass-by-space circulation route takes a U-shaped path around the central core, providing access to the consulting and treatment rooms organized around the perimeter of the plan. This clear strategy eliminates the confusion often caused by a labyrinthine system of corridors.

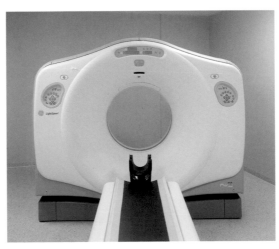

Left
The treatment rooms are organized in a clustered arrangement that takes advantage of the site's complex geometry of overlapping spaces.

Case Study Planning solutions

Shine boutique, Hong Kong / LEAD and NC Design & Architecture

Shine is a Hong Kong retailer that sells fashion collections from a variety of different brands. This project, completed in 2011 by LEAD and NC Design & Architecture, transforms a simple small shop unit into a boutique in which the necessary spaces are organized in an economical and intelligent way. The apparent simplicity of this clear configuration belies the plan's clever strategies for the spatial and circulation requirements of the programme. As in most successful interiors, a number of different strategies are employed here that enable the building to function as it should.

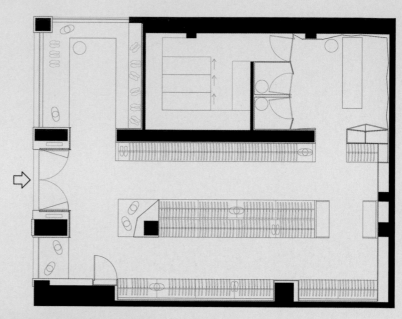

Above

The rectangular shop unit has been carefully planned as a series of six adjacent spaces that fit together to form a compact plan, making the most of the space offered by the site. The main shop floor and the cashier area act as common spaces to link other spaces; they both also have a pass-through-space circulation. Circulation routes terminate in the other four spaces – the shoe and bag area, the two fitting rooms and the storage area – and each of these spaces has an adjacent relationship with the common space to which it is connected.

Left

The main shop floor has a pass-through-space circulation and acts as a common space that links the two adjacent spaces.

Above
The shoe and bag area is located immediately to the left of the main shop-floor space, with which it has an adjacent spatial relationship. The circulation route terminates in this space, forcing the user to retrace their steps to exit.

Below
The cashier space has an adjacent relationship with the four spaces connected to it and a pass-through-space circulation, giving users access to the two fitting rooms (customers) and the storage area (staff) as well as allowing them to return to the main shop-floor space (customers and staff).

Below
Having passed through the length of the main shop-floor space, users can enter the adjacent cashier space that provides further access to the fitting rooms and the storage area.

CHAPTER 5
FROM BRIEF TO PROPOSAL

Introduction

Interior design projects are developed from a range of
different starting points, but sooner or later it is essential
for the requirements to be translated into a brief that sets
out the aims of the project and the scope of the work.
A brief is generally a written document that serves as the
start a journey through which thoughts, words, images
and experiences are formed into a built reality. This
complex process is not necessarily straightforward or
linear – each project will have its own specific character
and criteria, which will inform the processes required
to resolve its challenges. This chapter investigates the
ways in which a project brief can be developed into a
proposal for the spatial organization of an interior.

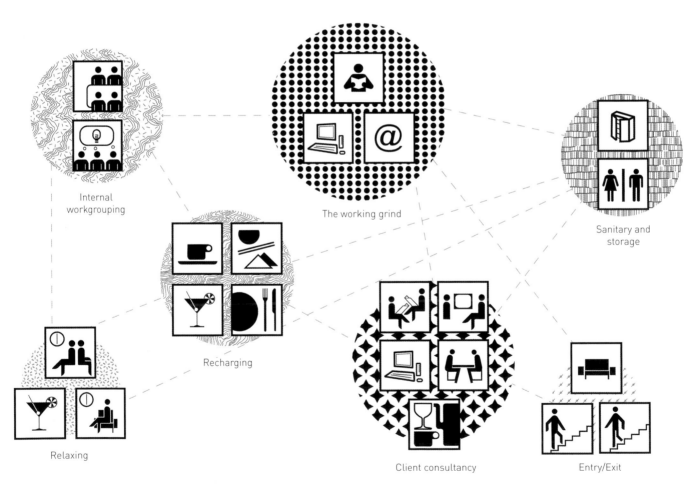

Internal
workgrouping

The working grind

Sanitary and
storage

Recharging

Relaxing

Client consultancy

Entry/Exit

Above
Studio SKLIM developed the
brief for their Thin Office
proposal (Singapore, 2010) into
a graphic diagram that begins
the process of investigating
the relationship of spaces.

The brief

Project briefs can be very different. Some clients have a very clear understanding of their area of activity and how it operates, and are able to give a precise and detailed brief (listing the required spaces and how they should relate/function) to the interior designer, whose job will then involve translating this information into a built reality that meets the client's requirements. Other clients wish to create an interior to enable a particular activity to take place but have no idea how this should happen. In this instance, the client engages the interior designer to analyze the problem and develop proposals as to how the activity might function.

Imagining, speculating and inventing

Many straightforward activities can be executed in different ways, the nature of which will have an impact on the people undertaking them and the spaces they require. The spatial organization of buildings is concerned with orchestrating how people undertake activities in an interior and ensuring that appropriate spaces are provided to allow this to happen.

There is a danger that an interior designer will simply replicate existing solutions when given a brief, without thinking about how a problem *could* be solved. Designers have a responsibility to dream, think and invent with a

Far left and left
Blacksheep's 2009 scheme for the Inamo restaurant in London, UK utilized digital technology to introduce a new ordering system that transforms the way in which the interior operates. Interactive menus are projected on to tabletops, allowing diners to order anything at any time without delay. This new approach provides customers with a novel experience while improving the operator's efficiency.

Left
Launched in 1997, the British YO! Sushi chain is known for its stimulating eating environments, based on the concept of a Japanese *kaiten* sushi bar. Chefs prepare food in a central space, surrounded by customers sitting at a bar. Once prepared, dishes are placed on a slowly rotating conveyor belt and diners can choose items as they move past. Coloured plates signify the price of each portion and the bill is determined by adding up the customer's stack of crockery.

view to creating new solutions that challenge and improve the status quo. One example of this is restaurant design: there are a number of well-established ways in which restaurants can function that are appropriate in different contexts. How the food is ordered and delivered (waiter service, self service or assisted service) and when and how payment is made (before or after consumption) will have a profound effect on the customers and staff using the space, as well as determining the interior's spatial organization

(the spaces required, their size and relationships). The interior designer's job may be to develop new ways in which the restaurant could operate, with the aim of providing a better user experience or creating a more efficient operating model in terms of staff, time or space.

An intelligent interior designer explores how an activity *could* be undertaken before making an informed decision as to how it should be done.

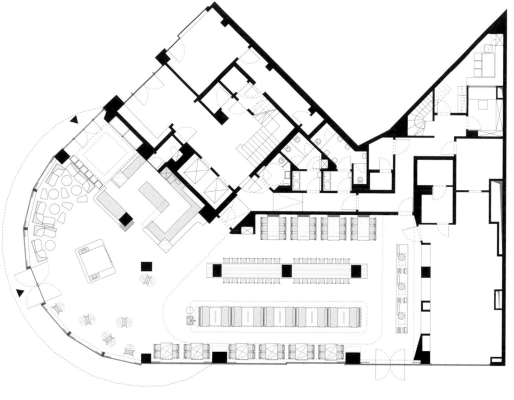

Above and above right

In 2010 Ippolito Fleitz Group created a new restaurant concept for Holyfields in Germany that delivers a quality dining environment at value prices. Customers use a touch screen to place their order and then take an electronic signaller to their seat. When the food is ready a signal is emitted and the customer collects the meal from a counter. This new service system has an impact on the spatial organization: more space is required at the entrance to accommodate the free-standing ordering terminals and a food-collection point must be established.

Right

Japan's Tokyo Curry Lab reinvents what a restaurant can be. Designed by Wonderwall in 2007, the venue is conceived as a laboratory, where customers are encouraged to feel as if they are part of a research team testing the food. A single dish is prepared each day, which, along with the seating arrangement, promotes the idea that the 30 diners are taking part in a conference and are involved in the scientific development of the recipe.

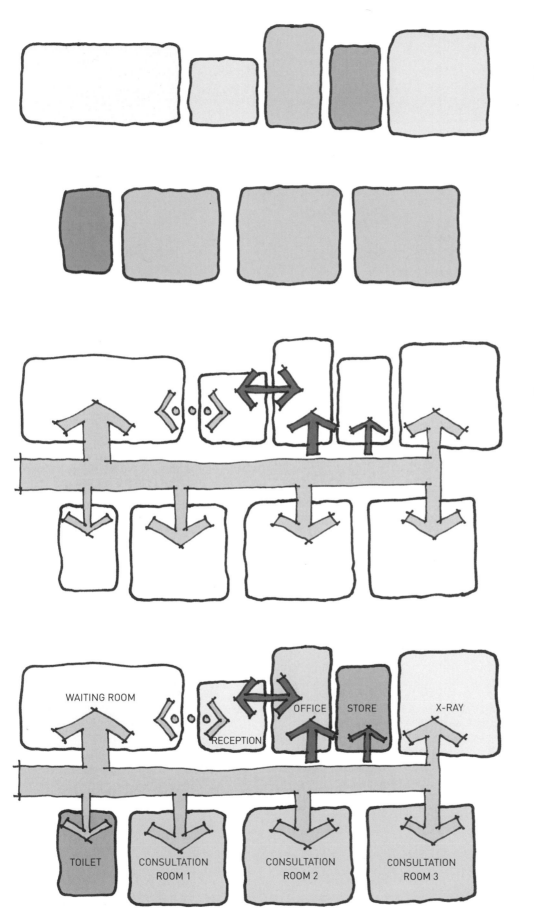

3 **Colour**: the diagram will have greater clarity if colour is used to assist communication. Choose colours carefully to reinforce the diagram's message: here, yellow signifies a space used only by patients, blues signify areas used only by staff and greens identify spaces used by both.

4 **Arrows**: connections between spaces can be explained using arrows. As before, colour can be used to identify different types of connection: here, patient/staff circulation is shown in light grey and circulation restricted to staff in dark grey. A dashed arrow indicates a visual connection between the reception and waiting areas.

5 **The finished diagram**: all the above elements are synthesized to create a final diagram that communicates the planning strategy quickly and clearly. The nature of the freehand drawing promotes the idea that the diagram is an informal communication of the principles behind the spatial arrangement – it is part of the design process rather than a finalized scheme.

WAITING ROOM

RECEPTION

OFFICE   STORE   X-RAY

TOILET   CONSULTATION ROOM 1   CONSULTATION ROOM 2   CONSULTATION ROOM 3

Case study Store

COS stores / William Russell, Pentagram

COS (Collection of Style) is a Swedish fashion brand that offers beautifully designed, well-made clothes at accessible prices. Known for its attention to detail, COS produces functional designs crafted from simple ideas and aspires to create clothing that is at once classic and modern. William Russell, a partner at design firm Pentagram in London, developed a concept for the company's retail outlets in 2007, based on the different collections that make up the larger COS brand. The men's and women's sections are each divided into four zones dedicated to a specific collection: Casual City, Classic, Leisure and Party. 'The idea for the store came from COS having smaller collections within a bigger collection. I started thinking about zones, which became rooms,' Russell explains.

The store's design is heavily influenced by mid-century modern Scandinavian design, a reflection of Russell's own love of that aesthetic and the client's corporate home in Sweden. Instead of dividing up the space with walls, Russell demarcated the areas with a thick black metal rail that runs throughout the store at a continuous height. A collection of display components were developed that work in conjunction with the rail, and the result is an interior planning proposal that is composed of a kit of parts that can be assembled in a variety of ways to suit any given site. These 'installations' consistently deliver the same conceptual idea in numerous sites that have different characters, spatial configurations and sizes.

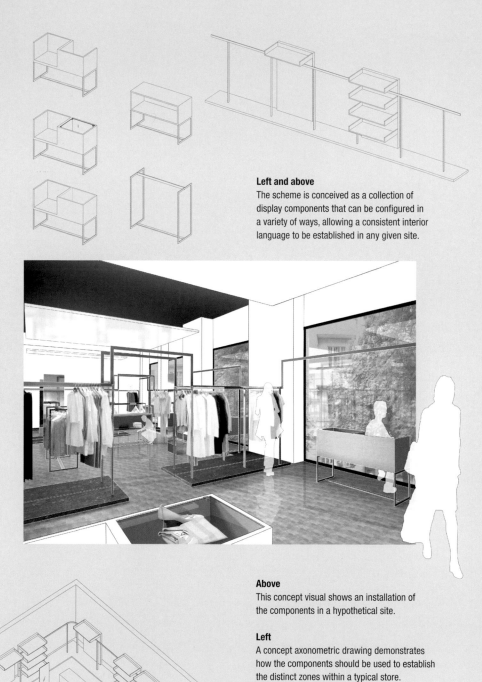

Left and above
The scheme is conceived as a collection of display components that can be configured in a variety of ways, allowing a consistent interior language to be established in any given site.

Above
This concept visual shows an installation of the components in a hypothetical site.

Left
A concept axonometric drawing demonstrates how the components should be used to establish the distinct zones within a typical store.

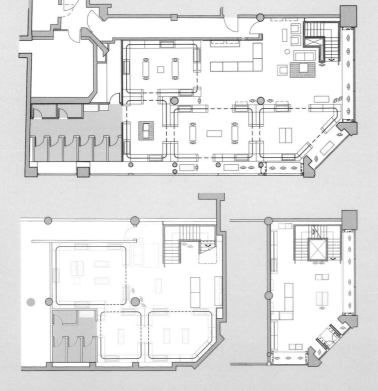

Left
At the site on Regent Street in London, UK the shop is arranged over the ground and first floors – both levels are of a similar size. The building is located at the junction of two streets and customers enter at the corner of the ground floor.

Left
Smaller than the site in London, the store in Hamburg, Germany comprises three levels. As in London, the entrance is at the corner of the site – here, customers arrive in a relatively small space on the ground floor, from where they can visit the main shopping area on the first floor and the additional space in the basement.

Planning diagrams

Having considered pertinent issues in isolation, the interior designer can synthesize the information gathered to produce a single diagram that establishes the appropriate spaces and their size, shape and relationships to each other. In addition there should, at this stage, be an understanding of the quality of space required for each activity – a need for daylight or separation, for example. The result is the planning diagram, which sets out the criteria that the interior's spatial organization must satisfy. As design work progresses and the interior's planning is developed, the designer should be able to test the spatial organization of the building against the planning diagram to ensure that the proposed scheme satisfies the required criteria.

Although the planning diagram is an important part of the design process, it is important to remember that it is not a building plan. Many different building plans can be developed from the same planning diagram. The final planning outcome will be determined by the qualities of the site and the conceptual aims of the project.

Below
A planning diagram combines information concerning the accommodation schedule, the relationship of spaces, and the size and shape of spaces.

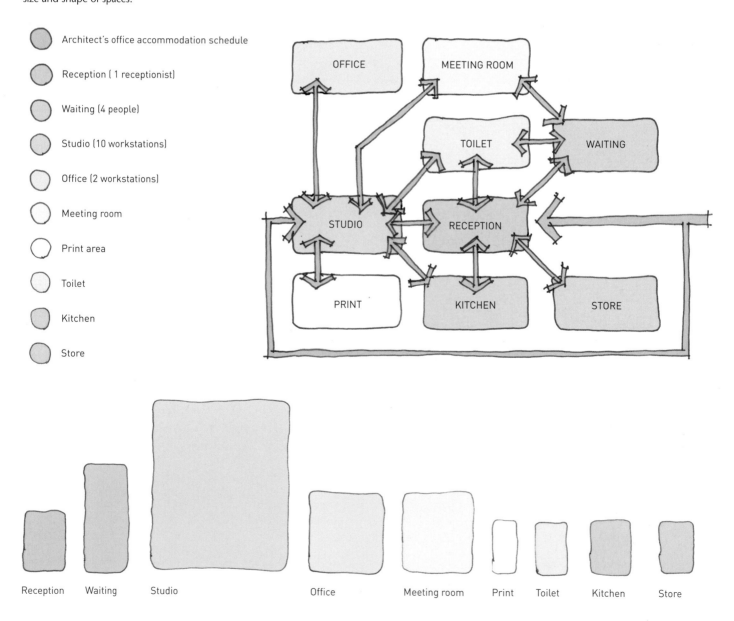

Architect's office accommodation schedule

Reception (1 receptionist)

Waiting (4 people)

Studio (10 workstations)

Office (2 workstations)

Meeting room

Print area

Toilet

Kitchen

Store

Above
The planning diagram establishes an ideal model of how the interior's spatial organization should work. It can be checked against the design process to ensure that each of the necessary spaces has been included and that their size, shape and relationship to each other will allow the building to function as required. If all these conditions are met by the completed interior, there is a good chance its organization will satisfy the aims and objectives of the project brief.

Relating the planning diagram to the site

The planning diagram records an ideal model for the way in which the interior should operate. It is, however, important to be aware that this information is purely diagrammatic – this is not the plan of an interior. In theory, an architect working with an open site could take the diagram and turn it into a built reality with few adjustments, but the interior designer's task is significantly different because their work takes place in the context of an existing site.

In order to progress a proposal, the planning diagram must be tested against the site in order to establish an acceptable relationship between the functional requirements of the brief and the qualities

Below and opposite
It is important to remember that the planning diagram is not a building plan. These drawings show a 2010 proposal by Spacesmith for fashion company Edun's showroom and offices in New York, USA – a planning diagram has been developed into a sketch layout that is in turn developed into the proposed interior plan.

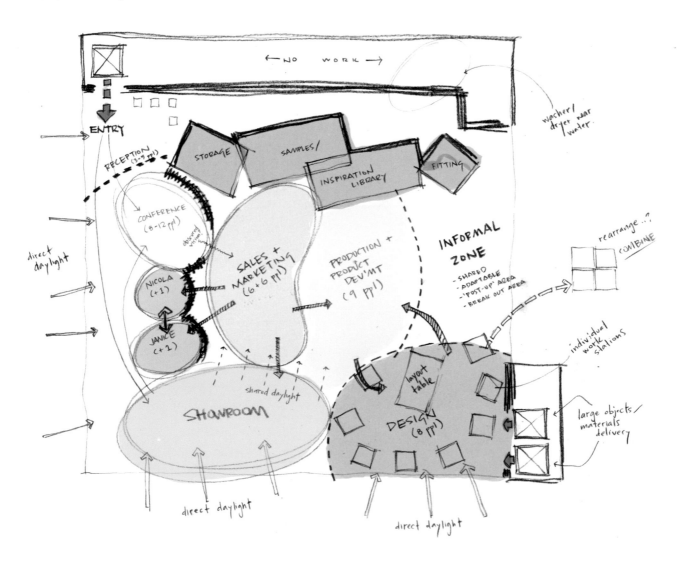

of the building in which the interior will be formed. This is relatively straightforward, as both the planning diagram and the plan drawing of the existing site can be at the same scale; 1:100 (or 1/8" = 1'-0") or 1:50 (or 1/4" = 1'-0") scales are often appropriate for the interior designer's work at this stage of a project. It is important to note that the same planning diagram can assume many different forms of layout without changing the relationships it has established – a variety of spatial organizations can be created in an existing space from the same starting point. Indeed, the interior designer should explore and test many options before making a decision as to the most appropriate layout.

As the planning diagram is an 'ideal' and the site is an existing building, there will inevitably be some compromise. Often the work of an interior designer is concerned with optimizing a situation that is far from perfect, and concessions must be made to accommodate an activity in the given space. Indeed, the qualities of some sites are so fixed – be it glazing, drainage or the position of the entrance – that these factors dominate the decision-making process rather than the ideal relationships established in the planning diagram.

This process should lead to the establishment of a sketch plan that reconciles the demands of the brief with the constraints of the existing site. The interior designer is then able to explore the way in which the plan can be articulated in three dimensions (see Chapter 7). Once decisions have been made, information can be recorded (and developed) in formal drawings of plans and sections of the scheme.

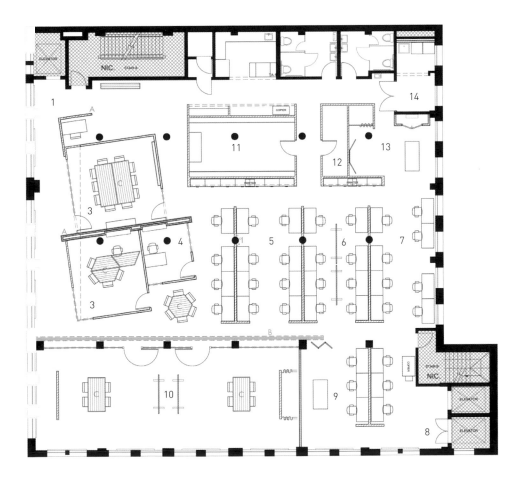

1 Reception
2 Conference room
3 CEO's office
4 CFO's office
5 Sales and marketing
6 Production workspace
7 Technical workplace
8 Freight entrance
9 Design workspace
10 Showroom
11 Sample room
12 Storage room
13 Fitting area
14 Wash and dye room

A Wall clad in reclaimed whitewashed wood
B Reclaimed whitewashed wood beam floating in front of glass wall
C Locally sourced custom-made reclaimed wood tables

A   B   C

Right
The qualities of the existing site will present opportunities and demand compromises. Factors such as the location of glazing, structural elements (including walls and columns) and existing entrances will help determine how the planning diagram is reconciled with the building fabric.

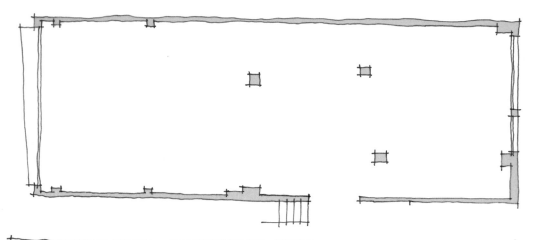

Right and below right
The same planning diagram (see pages 90 and 91) can be introduced to the site in many different ways. As the planning diagram has been drawn at a recognized scale, usually 1:100 (or 1/8" = 1'-0") or 1:50 (or 1/4" = 1'-0"), information can easily be tested against a plan of the existing building. Many options should be explored before the sketch plan is established.

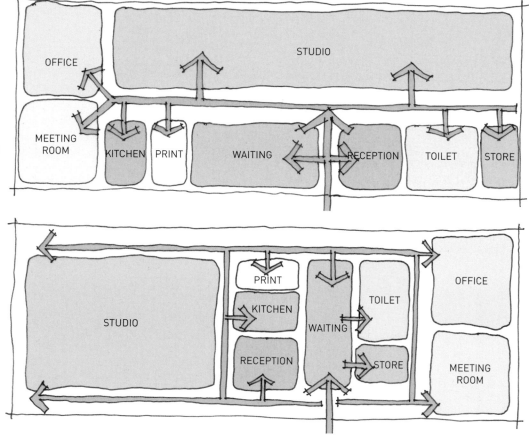

Right
Once the sketch plan has been explored in three dimensions, information can be recorded to produce the finished planning proposal. As the process progresses, more and more detail is resolved.

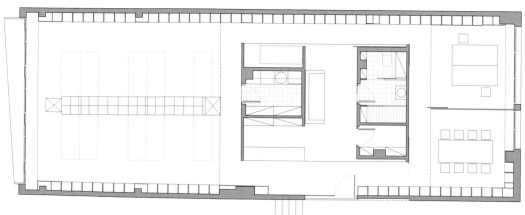

Left and below
Views of the completed interior
used as a case study – the
offices of B Mes R 29 Arquitectes
in Lleida, Spain (2008).

Case study Exhibition

'Rogers Stirk Harbour + Partners – From the House to the City' / Ab Rogers Design

The exhibition 'Rogers Stirk Harbour + Partners – From the House to the City' was originally installed at the Centre Pompidou in Paris, France in 2007. It was organized around key themes of the architecture firm's output: Early Work, Transparent, Lightweight, Legible, Green, Public, Systems, Urban and Work in Progress. Models were displayed on a family of irregularly shaped tables, with each theme identified by a different colour to code the different zones of the exhibition. A 60-metre (196-foot) timeline wall used drawings and photographic images to depict the work of the practice in a chronological sequence while a 'piazza' in the central area of the exhibition space provided visitors with the opportunity to read about the projects.

The coloured tables, timeline wall and the 'piazza' formed the component parts of the scheme. Designed as separate elements, they could be combined in different ways, which allowed the exhibition to be installed in a number of very different sites. Over a five-year period, the exhibition was shown in Barcelona, Beijing, Hong Kong, London, Madrid, Singapore and Taipei.

Above
The initial installation at the Pompidou Centre in Paris, France.

Below
One of the key elements of the exhibition was the long timeline wall, which had to be realized in a number of different situations.

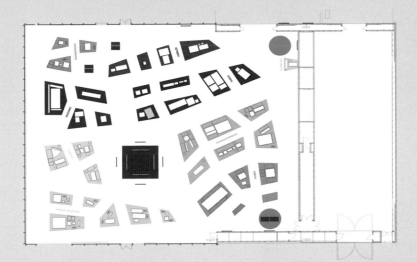

Above
The plan of the Pompidou Centre installation.

Below
Plans of subsequent installations in Barcelona, Madrid and Taipei illustrate how the same design concept was arranged in a variety of different layouts in response to the existing sites.

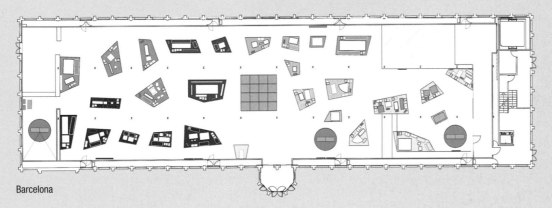

Barcelona

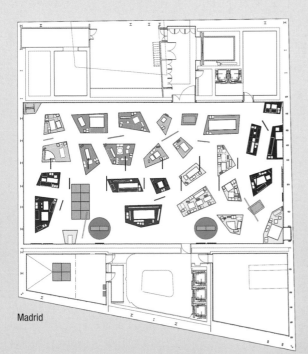

Madrid

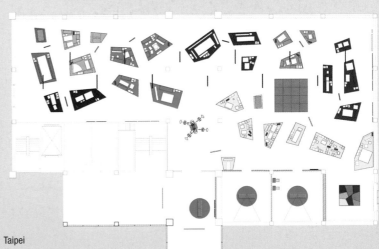

Taipei

CHAPTER 6
THE EXISTING BUILDING'S IMPACT

Introduction

The interior designer will generally work within an interior space and consequently an existing building will provide the context for the proposal. The envelope in which the work is to be done may be of great historical importance, full of ornate architectural detail or a simple, empty retail unit in a new shopping centre. No matter how grand or mundane the context, it will always necessitate some thought as to how something new should be juxtaposed against the existing environment. The response to this question is key to a project's success and provides the interior designer with an enjoyable challenge.

This chapter will introduce issues the designer should consider when analyzing an existing building and go on to identify strategies they can employ to introduce the new interior.

Above and left
To celebrate the fiftieth anniversary of the art gallery at Duivenvoorde Castle in the Netherlands, the 'Portrait Pavilion' designed by Pauline Bremmer Architects in collaboration with Office Jarrik Ouburg was placed in the building's eighteenth-century ballroom in 2010. The form of the new object's plan responds to the pattern of the room's carpet and a contrast is established between the highly decorative existing interior and the new, minimal mirrored box.

Analyzing an existing building

The ability to analyze and understand an existing building improves with knowledge and experience. Buildings are complex and there is much to learn about why and how any particular structure was built, as well as the way in which it presents itself to the interior designer who is contemplating working within it. The following pages outline a number of different issues to consider when developing an understanding of a site. However, the particular nature of the building in question will dictate which of these issues are pertinent at any given time. Information acquired as a result of this process will be of vital importance – the development of the design scheme is often a direct response to issues identified during the analysis. The interior designer must evaluate what might be worth analyzing in order to gain an understanding that will assist the project's development.

Left
The **site** consists of a warehouse building dating from the late nineteenth century, located on Lower John Street at the south-western corner of Golden Square in Soho, London, UK.

Left
The **location** is clearly identified in these aerial photographs, which give some visual clues as to the nature of its context. Here, an understanding is gained that the site (outlined in red) is located in a dense urban context, to the edge of a public square and close to a main artery.

Bottom left
In the UK, Ordnance Survey maps at a scale of 1:1250 (approximately 50 inches to 1 mile) are used to communicate factual information about a building's precise location. Here, the site in question is clearly indicated by a red outline, the footprints of adjacent buildings are identified and the site's relationship with its surroundings can begin to become more apparent.

Left
The **history** of the site and how the immediate environment has evolved over a period of time can often be appreciated through the analysis of old photographs and illustrations.

This section is illustrated with material from a single project, 20 Golden Square and 5 Lower John Street in central London, UK. Originally built in the 1880s and now used as office space, this former warehouse underwent various alterations during the nineteenth and twentieth centuries and is currently in need of substantial repair and modernization. In 2013, the architectural practice Orms undertook a feasibility study to evaluate how the building could be developed.

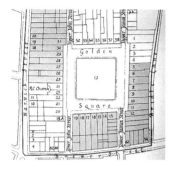

Above
Local archives hold material such as maps from different periods, which are vital tools to further understanding an area's development over a number of years.

Right and far right
The **access** routes to a site can influence interior planning decisions. Here, a one-way traffic system means that vehicles can only make an oblique approach from the left and in a frontal manner to the corner of the site, while pedestrian access is from the left, right and in front of the portion of the building that faces into the square. The site's relationship to the nearest Underground station means that, in the morning, pedestrians mainly approach the building from the left while this is reversed in the evening.

Right
The **orientation** of the building will affect how and when daylight enters the spaces. Here, east-facing windows have blinds to protect the room's users from the early morning sun.

Left

A building's **construction** type will inform decisions as to how it might be altered. Here, load-bearing brick walls combine with cast-iron columns and timber beams to support timber floors. Within the structural grid, apertures could be formed in the floors with relative ease but removing columns and beams would be more challenging.

Below

An awareness of the type, number and location of **openings** in a building will assist the designer when developing the interior scheme. One of building's two entrances from the street was modified in the 1960s but an original arched window remains above it and has a significant impact on the interior space beyond.

Above

The **materials** of the existing building will inform design decisions. Here, some exploratory work undertaken on an existing staircase reveals how the timber will look following refurbishment.

Above

The **condition** of the existing interior will often inform the proposal. An existing timber floor displays wear patterns that are related to the positions of machinery that has long since been removed.

Above

An understanding of the **architectural detail** in a building will allow the interior designer to make informed decisions in response. Here, the capital of a neoclassical column has been established in the Tuscan order.

Above

The integration of **services** into existing buildings is complex: here, electrical and heating services have been added to the building in a rather ad hoc manner. A sensitive refurbishment will demand new installations.

Right
Floor spaces and volumes
must be suitable for the activities proposed for them. Here, a large, dramatic, top-lit volume is interrupted by a grid of columns, making for a space that is difficult to subdivide into smaller spaces. The interior designer will need to carefully consider how this fantastic open volume can be utilized to its full potential.

Right
The building's **structural grid** can drive the planning solution. Here, the main elements of the building are arranged according to a rectangular network of columns (shown in red) that relate to the top and right-hand side of the plan. The building's facade responds to this grid, while the irregular perimeter to the left and bottom of the plan responds to the form of the adjacent buildings.

Far right
In many interior situations, established **circulation** routes can be difficult to alter and will therefore influence future planning decisions. Here, an existing staircase is of architectural interest, suggesting that it should be retained as an integral part of the proposed interior scheme.

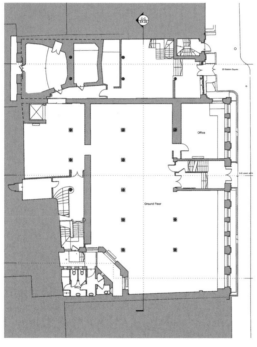

Right
An understanding of the host building will help the designer identify **opportunities for change**. Here, an appreciation of the building's construction type, the structural grid and the openings establish a proposal to create a void between floors that would allow daylight to penetrate from the roof lights to the level below.

Introducing new into existing

Once the interior designer has analyzed the existing building and developed some understanding of the site, they will consider how any new interior elements will be introduced. While the approach may be influenced by the nature of the client, the needs of the building programme, the proposed lifespan of the interior and the project's budget, for an interior designer the response to the existing is of paramount importance. The designer will consider how the given building fabric should be treated (restored, preserved, conserved or refurbished), as well as how any newly introduced component will relate to that which exists. They can choose to set up dynamic contrast between the old and new or create a seamless transition from the past to the future.

In their book *Re-readings: Interior Architecture and the Design Principles of Remodelling Existing Buildings*, Graeme Brooker and Sally Stone set out three strategies for introducing a new interior to an existing building:

- **Intervention**
- **Insertion**
- **Installation**

These strategies offer clear and intelligent approaches as to how the interior designer can consider the relationship between a new interior and the existing building within which it is housed. As a relatively new discipline, interior design has only an emerging theoretical base from which to operate and, as a result, designers often use terms such as 'installation' and 'insertion' to describe what can be contradictory approaches to similar problems. For the sake of clarity and consistency, this book will use the terms established by Brooker and Stone as a helpful means of defining strategies an interior designer might employ in response to an existing building.

Below

Pardo + Tapia Arquitectos' scheme for the El Greco Museum in Toledo, Spain was completed in 2012. In the remains of a sixteenth-century house, new 'floating' walkways are introduced that take visitors on a journey through the historic spaces without touching them.

This page
In 2013 a former factory in Turin, Italy was turned into a contemporary office space for IT company Sempla. DAP Studio decided to strip back the existing building fabric while retaining traces of the structure's past before introducing crisp white elements that establish a strong dialogue between old and new.

Far left
The new interior enables visual connections to be made between different floor levels within the space. Apertures in the existing building fabric respond to the new interior configuration, setting up a playful tension between inside and outside, the old and the new.

Left
Worktop, wall and balustrade fuse together to become abstract spatial forms that have a bold simplicity that contrasts with the original building fabric.

Left
Traces of the original staircase are left exposed, providing information about the building's past.

Below left and right
Sometimes new interior components float away from the old building fabric, at other times they gently meet and on occasion the new crashes through the old. Whatever the approach employed, great importance is placed on the relationship between the original architecture and the new interior.

Insertion

According to Graeme Brooker and Sally Stone, an insertion happens when 'the host building allows and accommodates new elements, which are built to fit the exact dimensions of the existing, to be introduced in or around it yet remains very much unchanged'.[2]

Deploying an insertion strategy can establish a conversation between an existing building and the newly introduced elements. This exchange will often be cordial, as the new components are tailor-made for the particular site and may assume a form that is identical to or in sympathy with the original building. Although the new insertion may be specifically designed for a particular location, it could still provide an opportunity for conflict by assuming a form that is quite contradictory to the existing space. The host building can remain completely unchanged during the work or it can be modified prior to the introduction of the tailored components.

As this strategy means there is a direct relationship between the size of the insertion and the space into which it is introduced, the result is a bespoke interior solution that is designed to exist in a single place. Although they are not intended to be relocated, the inserted elements can be removed without unduly affecting the structure they inhabit.

2 Brooker and Stone, *Re-readings*, p. 79.

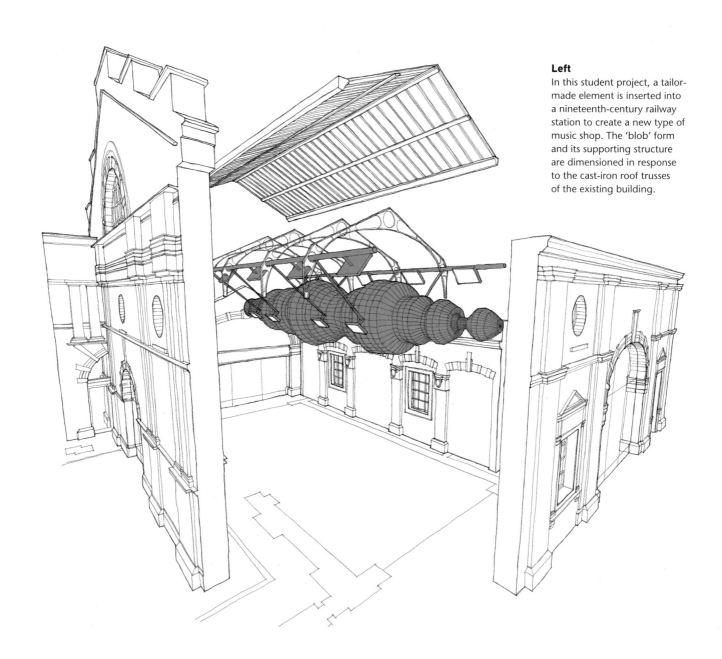

Left
In this student project, a tailor-made element is inserted into a nineteenth-century railway station to create a new type of music shop. The 'blob' form and its supporting structure are dimensioned in response to the cast-iron roof trusses of the existing building.

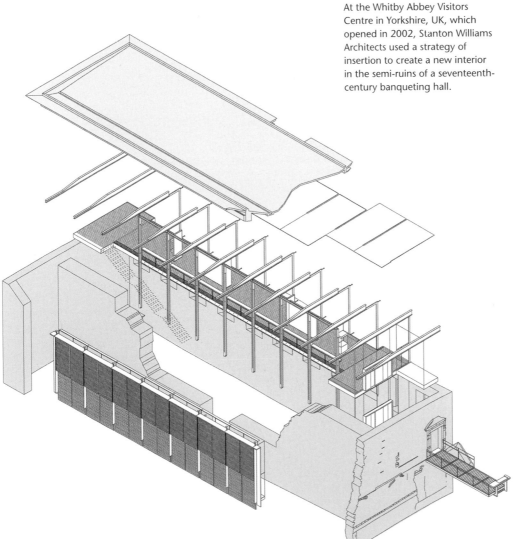

Above
At the Whitby Abbey Visitors Centre in Yorkshire, UK, which opened in 2002, Stanton Williams Architects used a strategy of insertion to create a new interior in the semi-ruins of a seventeenth-century banqueting hall.

Below left
A tailor-made steel structure that supports a roof and an upper floor level is inserted into the ruin, so that it reads as an independent modern structure that contrasts with the existing stone remains. On the southern elevation, a metal, glass and timber wall hangs like a curtain from the structure to provide an enclosure that further emphasizes the juxtaposition of new against old.

Case study Insertion

Silence Room at Selfridges department store, London, UK / Alex Cochrane Architects

An 'insertion' involves placing new elements in an existing space in such a way that it would be possible to remove them later without having any impact on the original building. What makes this strategy distinct from an 'installation' (see next page) is that the dimensions of the new elements are a direct response to the measurements of the existing site, meaning that the new interior is tailor-made for the particular site it sits within.

Alex Cochrane Architects employed a strategy of insertion in response to the parameters of this project, which was completed in 2013. As the Silence Room was a temporary interior, it was important that the space could be established and then removed, leaving the existing building intact. The site presented a space that contained six columns, which could have been considered problematic but ultimately drove the solution.

By wrapping a thick wall around the columns, a central room is created that sits within the existing volume. This tactic responds to the programme – to create a silent space – by forming a destination that is isolated from the main shop floor by the void surrounding it. In this instance, an insertion provides an intelligent solution to the challenges established by the proposed lifespan of the interior, the site context and the programme.

This scheme confidently executes a big conceptual idea to great effect. A decision was made to treat the host space as a 'black box' and introduce a new rectilinear volume as a 'space within a space'. The outside of the new box is dark, helping to create a gloomy circulation path that eventually arrives at the warmly lit, soft sanctuary at the heart of the space. All the new elements are dimensioned to unify the existing.

Right and below right
Initial conceptual drawings show the proposal as a light-box that floats in the existing dark volume as 'a space within a space'. The void between the building and the inserted object becomes the circulation space, forcing users on a spiralling journey that works its way around the box before terminating in the Silence Room itself.

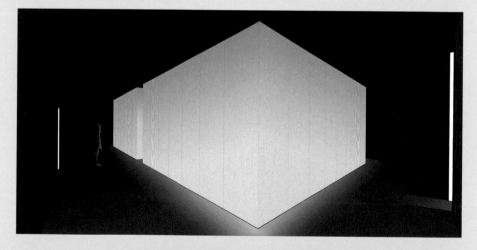

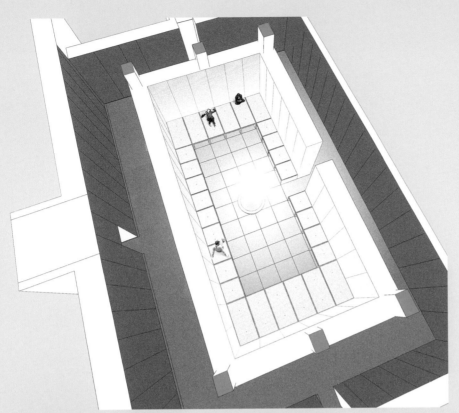

Left
The simple planning diagram has to resolve some challenges set by the site, where there are six existing columns (highlighted in red) in the given space. The sizes and positions of the columns are considered and the solution then uses this information as the determining factor for the dimensions of the inserted box. The designers made the decision to create the central room with an outer and inner skin, which gives the impression of a thick wall defining the central space and means the existing columns can be 'lost' in a cavity. The result is a structure that is tailor-made for this location in response to the particular content and dimensions of the site.

Left and far left
The existing space is painted black to create a mysterious intermediate space between the busy department store and the sanctuary of the Silence Room. Users circulate around the central volume in near darkness before arriving in the softly lit, tranquil destination space. MDF panels line the walls of the existing building and form the outer skin of the central volume, thus creating a smooth, hard circulation zone. Each panel is tailor-made for the specific dimensions of the site.

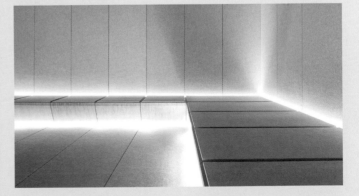

Above
The central space presents itself as a safe haven that contrasts with the preceding circulation route and the shop floor beyond. Gentle lighting suggests that the space is 'floating', while the walls, seating and floor are clad with soft felt panels, providing comfort and acoustic absorption. The central volume is open above and 'borrows' the ceiling of the existing space. Existing services are left exposed but are painted black.

Above
For this temporary interior with a lifespan of a few months, a limited palette of simple materials is used, but they are detailed with care and precision to produce a refined result. Natural wool felt and oak veneer are utilzed in a rigorous manner, working strictly to a grid used to rationalize the architectural elements of the existing site.

Installation

According to Graeme Brooker and Sally Stone, an installation occurs when 'the old and the new exist together but very little rapport between them is established'.[3] When employing a strategy of installation, the interior designer might place new objects in an existing building that has been left exactly as it was found. This can lead to an interesting dialogue between new and old elements in terms of materials and finish – a smooth, glossy new object might be set in a roughly textured old interior. It may be the case that a programme of restoration, refurbishment or renovation is carried out first and that, once work on the host building has been completed, the space is ready for new pieces to be installed.

In terms of size, all that is required is that the existing building is large enough to accommodate the new installation. As an installation strategy means there is little relationship between the host structure and the newly introduced interior elements, this approach is often used for temporary exhibitions and events where

Below

Completed in 2008, the offices of the Pullpo advertising agency in Santiago, Chile were designed by Hania Stambuk. Glass and steel objects were installed in the cavernous volume of a disused salt factory to create more intimate spaces. The new elements are dimensioned to respond to the activities they house and have no direct relationship with the size or form of the architectural envelope.

a lightness of touch is required. For touring events, a modular structure can be assembled in a particular configuration in one site and then assume a different form that is suitable for another site. This approach can be adopted for retail design, where a set of components could be designed to give a particular brand an interior identity, with the intention that these elements could then be assembled and arranged in a variety of ways to respond to different site conditions. In both these circumstances, one key to the success of the strategy will be the consideration of tolerance: it is vital to ensure that the relationship between the installation and the host building is loose and 'baggy'. Additionally, it is important to consider the way in which the newly installed elements sit within the existing building – like a piece of furniture in a room, the relationship is temporary. Once removed, little trace should be left behind.

3 Brooker and Stone, *Re-readings*, p. 79.

Top left

Gundry & Ducker designed The Draughtsman's Arms as part of a short exhibition and debate on the future of architecture, which took place in the crypt of a church in London, UK designed by Sir John Soane. This small-scale project comprised a hanging object that was installed in the space, which served as the reception area for the exhibition and then as a bar during the debate. Once the exhibition was over, the structure was removed and the building left untouched.

Above

At the Wapping Project in London, UK (2000), the original hydraulic power station is left almost untouched and the restaurant is established by placing the interior elements as pieces of furniture. The new contrasts with the old and could be removed at any time, leaving the original architecture intact.

Case study Installation

KMS Team studio, Munich, Germany / Tools Off.Architecture

Left

The condition of the existing structure is preserved and the slightly decaying fabric of the disused industrial building retained. Existing folding timber doors open to reveal new glazed elements that are inserted into the existing apertures to create a weathertight interior volume, which is then defined by a series of objects installed in the space.

Below left

The existing interior is treated in a simple manner, with a functional aesthetic appropriate to the building's original use. A robust, understated shell is created that will contain new interior elements.

Below centre

Where a need to connect existing levels arises, an industrial staircase is installed as an 'object' that is independent of the building fabric. This staircase can be seen as a separate prefabricated entity that could happily exist elsewhere.

Below

A simple blackboard provides a flexible method of sharing information within the company. Located next the refreshment area, it can be used as a menu board or an office planning chart as required. The dimensions of the plane are determined by the sheet size of the material (as opposed to the wall behind it) and the blackboard leans casually against the building fabric, emphasizing its temporary nature compared to the static architecture.

For a project to be considered an 'installation', it needs to involve the positioning of interior elements whose size and form are considered in their own right and do not have a direct relationship with the dimensions or form of the host building. These elements, or objects, could be removed from the building and placed in another interior space of appropriate size and function just as well.

Completed in 2000 by the German practice Tools Off.Architecture, this project uses the strategy of installation to define the interior of a creative studio's workplace in a redundant industrial space. In a fine example of this approach, a number of new elements are installed in the space. Responding to the functional aesthetic of the industrial building, the designers utilized a simple palette of straightforward, hard-wearing raw materials that together provide a coherent language for the scheme. Timber, metal and concrete are used to define particular activities and a collection of objects is placed in the space to support the users' needs. Each object adopts a bold, confident form to ensure it clearly exists within the architectural space.

One of strengths of this scheme is the consideration given to how the existing site should be treated. A careful programme of preservation captures the industrial building's decaying condition, providing the perfect backdrop for the new forms the designers have introduced, which can be seen as sculptures in an art gallery. The relationship of the new and the old is temporary – the sculptures can be removed from the gallery at any time.

Above and above right
Specific interior functions are defined by folded planes of robust materials that respond to the qualities of the existing building. The dimensions of these planes are established by the requirements of the functions they cater for and have no relationship with the surrounding environment. A plane of folded rusting metal defines the library, while a folding concrete plane creates a space for a communal refreshment area. Contrasting materials establish the different functions of the spaces, while a common formal language unites the elements as part of a compositional whole.

Right and far right
The library space and the refreshment area both 'float' in the existing volume. The relationship between the new elements and the existing architecture makes a clear statement about the temporary nature of the interior in relation to the more permanent host building.

CHAPTER 7
DEVELOPING THREE-DIMENSIONAL SPATIAL COMPOSITIONS

Introduction

In essence, space planning is concerned with ensuring that spaces of the appropriate size, shape and type are located in the right place. For a building to function well, it is essential to achieve the correct arrangement of facilities. However, articulating this planning diagram in three dimensions provides a designer with the opportunity to create exciting and stimulating interior spaces suitable for the activities taking place in them. Any given planning arrangement can be realized in three dimensions in countless ways, allowing the interior designer to explore how materials, form and structure can be manipulated to create volumetric compositions that bring a planning diagram to life. This chapter will introduce issues concerning the development of three-dimensional spatial compositions as part of the interior design process.

Above

At the Combiwerk 'social workplace' in Delft, 2012, the Dutch design practice i29 defined different zones in an open space through the use of colour, compositions of vertical planes, changes in floor finish and the placement of furniture.

This approach created a sophisticated series of spaces that overlap and interconnect – they are sometimes private and at other times communal. The scheme explores the 'grey' areas of how space can be divided.

Above

The counter of the Pleats Please Issey Miyake shop in New York, USA is established by a floating cube installed in the site as a 'space within a space'. As the cube does not touch the floor, it immediately questions the idea of a spatial division (wall) that is traditionally built from the ground up. The faces that define the object as a cubic form are articulated in different ways, exploring thickness and how they can be more 'open' or 'closed', to create a volume that is both sculptural and functional. The shop was designed by Curiosity in 1999.

Right

Breathe Architecture completed the Captain Melville restaurant and bar in Melbourne, Australia in 2012. The dining space is an extension to an 1853 building that was the city's first hotel, and the seating and tables are defined by open metal frames whose form suggests the tent structures that the city's earliest settlers lived in. These elements contrast with the way in which both the new extension and the existing building have been established.

Defining space

Probably the most common task for an interior designer is determining how two adjacent spaces can be articulated as being different. This difference is frequently established through the construction of an opaque, floor-to-ceiling partition wall, leading to the creation of cellular box-like rooms. Although appropriate in many circumstances, this essentially rather unsophisticated and heavy-handed means of separation is not ideal in situations where more ambiguous ways of dividing space are infinitely more desirable. A full-height opaque partition wall provides an essentially 'closed' division of two adjacent spaces, while a line drawn on the floor is perhaps the most 'open' way of dividing one space into two. In terms of spatial division, these two examples represent the 'black and white' extremes of the spectrum. For an interior designer, the real interest lies in the 'grey area' in between, which provides infinite opportunities to explore how spaces can be divided in more or less 'open' or 'closed' ways. Developing interesting ways to establish spaces as being different involves investigating materials, form and structure, and this question alone could occupy a lifetime's work for an interior designer.

This page
In the top left image, a simple square space is divided in two by a line on the floor; in the bottom right image, a fully enclosed box establishes one half of the space as different to the other. Between these two extremes are examples of more ambiguous ways in which spaces can be defined as being distinct from each other – the possibilities are endless, and the development of these methods is a major part of the interior designer's work.

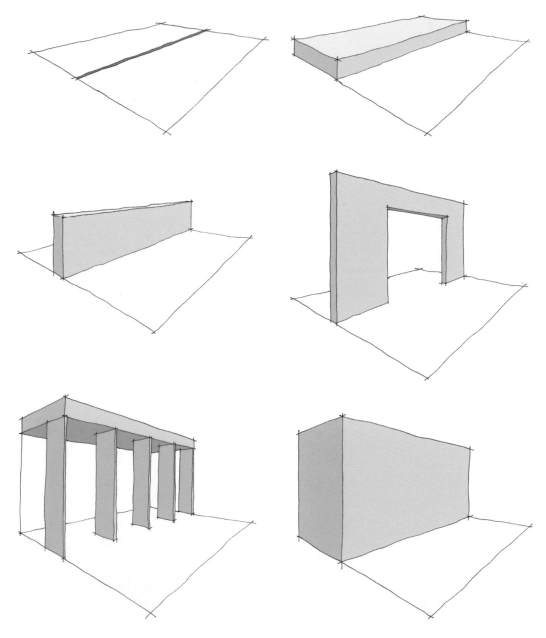

Case study Forming spatial compositions

Glass House, New Canaan, USA / Philip Johnson

Built in 1949, the Glass House is a collection of simple, pure geometric forms arranged to create a composition that defines the spaces necessary for a weekend retreat. In this small-scale building, a number of different spatial devices are used to establish the architectural envelope and the interior. Philip Johnson said that the inspiration for the building came from observing a burnt-out timber building, where all that remained were the brick foundations and the chimney. The form of the Glass House is defined by two brick elements: the elevated horizontal base plane and the cylinder containing the chimney and the bathroom. The interior is established when the overhead plane is located above the base plane and a steel cage with a glass skin is wrapped around the perimeter. The brick cylinder is conceived as a 'space within a space', allowing it to be perceived as a pure object in the interior, whose position has been carefully determined to help establish the primary division of the space into a series of interconnected zones. Within these zones, activities are defined by vertical and horizontal planes in the form of architectural elements, interior elements or pieces of furniture that all play their own considered role in the totality that is the finished composition.

As the Glass House is one of the twentieth century's most significant buildings, it is interesting to note that it can be read as an interior that blends into the landscape so successfully that the architecture is almost invisible. The elements that define the building belong to the interior designer's world – floor, ceiling, cupboard, kitchen unit, rug, painting, chair, table and bowl – and here they are composed with immense discipline and rigour.

Above
The Glass House is an essay in Modernist spatial composition that allows a series of separate zones to be defined in an open, interconnected manner. Even the position of the bowl on the table is considered as a part of the composition, playfully referencing the building's plan.

Above
Horizontal planes are among the devices used to articulate the building as a whole, defining different interior zones as well as activities within those zones.

Above
A series of vertical planes of different heights divide spaces so that they are more or less open to each other. These elements are more often pieces of furniture than walls.

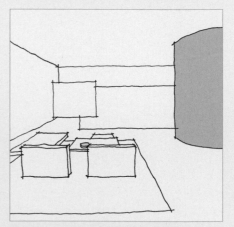

Above
Made from the same brick as the ground plane, the cylinder containing the chimney and bathroom is a 'space within a space', carefully placed in order to articulate the spaces between it and the glazed envelope. The cylinder's size, form and material make it the principal element of the house.

Exploring contrasts

Compositions of space can be defined in interesting, unusual and stimulating ways by exploring the opportunities to create contrasts between the elements in the configuration. There are many contrasts the interior designer can play with, including those between old and new, light and dark, smooth and textured, shiny and matt. By investigating the extremes of contrast – and as much of the grey area in between as possible – interior designers can achieve spatial compositions that have balance, harmony, or counterpoint where necessary. Perhaps the most important contrasts that an interior designer will explore in their work are:

- **Open versus closed**
- **Heavy versus light**
- **Opaque versus transparent**

These contrasts are concerned with the formal manner in which spaces are defined and relate to each other, as well as with the materials used in the process. Many successful interior schemes will create volumetric compositions that are defined by elements that explore all these contrasts simultaneously when establishing an interior space – indeed they are so interconnected that, at times, it might not be possible to separate one quality from another.

Left
In this private residence of 2012 in San Francisco, USA designers Garcia Tamjidi Architecture Design form divisions of space that are intended to be read as being simple, solid and 'closed'.

Left
The entrance to the Tribeca men's hair salon in Tokyo, Japan plays with ideas about inside and outside. Designed by Curiosity in 2006, the space is read as a whole but is divided in half by a glass partition: the interior is physically closed from the exterior but visually open. The form of the reception desk protrudes outside, while the entrance matting helps define the point of entry in an open way through a simple contrast of materials and colour – the black rectangle acts as a bridge from the outside to the inside (it also solves the practical problems created by hard floor finishes and wet weather conditions). Finally, a formal game is established in which the door (to be opened) is solid while the (closed) partition it sits in is translucent.

Open versus closed

As described above, spaces can be defined in an infinite number of ways which, at one extreme or the other, are completely open or completely closed. In between these two extremes lie endless variants that play with the idea of being more or less open or closed.

The size and form of an element used to define one space from another will be key in how much separation is created between two spaces. A full-height rectangular partition made of an opaque material will create a 'closed' division of space. If an aperture is formed in the partition, the division becomes less 'closed' and more 'open'. As the size or number of apertures is increased, the partition will become more and more 'open'. The material used to create the division of space is another contributing factor: when transparent, translucent or perforated materials are introduced, spaces can be physically divided (and therefore 'closed' from each other) but visually or acoustically connected (and therefore 'open' to each other). The appropriate level of physical or visual connection between different spaces will be determined by the functional requirements and, perhaps also, by the conceptual idea that underpins the scheme.

Left
These offices for a building company in San Francisco, USA were created in 2013 by jones | haydu. Workspaces are defined by timber dwarf walls that help to establish 'closed' personal space while allowing easy 'open' communication between colleagues above them.

Left
The Wonder Room at Selfridges department store in London is a collection of luxury brand boutiques. In 2007, Klein Dytham Architecture designed the interior, creating an elegant wall of fins running around the perimeter of the room. Seen head-on, the arrangement of the fins leaves the concession stores behind them very open, but when seen obliquely, the fins become a screen behind which the brands disappear and the focus turns to the central area of the room.

This page
A pivoting panel allows this partition in an apartment in Berlin, Germany designed by Reinhardt Jung in 2010 to become a flexible division of space – it can be arranged in a number of ways to create different levels of separation.

Light versus heavy

The interior designer can explore and manipulate form and material in order to introduce visual contrasts of 'weight' in spatial compositions. 'Lightness' and 'heaviness' can be achieved through the proportion and dimensions of elements, their texture, their colour and the materials used in their construction. A solid, opaque, thick, matt, rough, darkly coloured wall will be perceived as heavy while one that is transparent, thin, shiny, smooth and light in colour will have a lightness in comparison. An interior specialist can consciously design each element to contribute to the spatial composition as a whole. Conceptual ideas and functional needs will help determine the visual language the designer develops for the scheme.

Above

Dear Design's 2009 interior for the Lurdes Bergada & Syngman Cucala flagship store in Barcelona, Spain involves elements that explore contrasts in weight. The garments hang on elegant lightweight rails but the building fabric is dark and heavy, while the irregular, faceted wall that defines the shop's functional spaces is created in timber and fills the middle ground of the composition.

Right

Menswear designer Michel Brisson's boutique is located in a brutalist 1970s bank building in Montreal, Canada. Saucier + Perrotte Architectes 2011 design exposes the heaviness of the original concrete structure and sets it against the lightness of the new back-lit translucent ceiling, while smoked glass and mirrored finishes add elements of intermediate weight to the composition.

Above

The composition of this office building's lobby is defined by three elements: there is a 'light' glossy white envelope, within which sit two rectilinear banks of lifts (elevators) that are clad in a dark grey textured stone, creating a 'heavy' contrast. The soft, curvaceous and colourful lobby seating, which acts as a counterpoint to the monochromatic architecture, makes up the third component of group8's 2012 design for the Indochine Plaza Hanoi in Vietnam.

Right

At The Café in the Park in Osaka, Japan a composition of floating linear lighting fixtures creates a lightweight counterpoint to the heavier planes used to define the space as a whole. The project was designed by Curiosity in 2009.

Opaque versus transparent

The levels of opacity and transparency in an interior are generally determined by the materials used to establish the division of space. There are many materials that are completely opaque and some that offer high levels of transparency, such as glass and acrylic. For the interior designer, there is much to explore in the area between these two extremes. Translucency allows for the passage of light through a material while restricting visibility. The perception of a material's transparency or translucency will often depend on the prevailing lighting conditions: reflective tinted glass can become wholly transparent as the illumination is altered, allowing for the intriguing possibility of spaces changing from a transparent ('open') condition to an opaque ('closed') condition at the flick of a switch.

Above
In this 2012 design for an office building in Tianjin, China by Vector Architects, the meeting room is defined by a partition wall made of orange glass. The translucent nature of the material allows the brightly lit room to act as a giant light-fitting, illuminating the dark space surrounding it.

Below
Completed in 1986, John Pawson's central London shop for fashion company Jigsaw established a composition using the opacity of the building fabric, the translucent etched glass panels and the opaque timber display fixtures.

Above
A glass partition at the McAllen Public Library in Texas, USA is completely transparent below seated eye level but translucent above, providing glimpses into the space while maintaining some privacy for those relaxing inside it. This project was created in 2011 by MSR.

Above

As part of their 2000 scheme for the offices of the ARB (Architects Registration Board) in London, UK, dRMM created a central island 'hub' of meeting spaces defined by a translucent corrugated polycarbonate wall. The material's profile adds to the variety of views afforded by its transparency. The vertical partition contrasts with the opacity of the horizontal floor and ceiling planes.

Left

Curiosity's 1999 scheme for the Pleats Please Issey Miyake shop in New York, USA uses a glass treatment that offers changing degrees of transparency as visitors move around the interior.

Forming spatial compositions

An interior designer developing a spatial composition is rather like a chef preparing a meal: they combine a number of ingredients in a particular way to create a dish that contains a variety of aromas, flavours, textures and colours. In order to start work, the interior designer needs some ingredients to manipulate and combine towards a three-dimensional outcome. In purely compositional terms, there are some fundamental elements that form the basis of much interior design work. These can be identified as follows:

- **Horizontal planes**
- **Vertical planes**
- **Beams**
- **Columns**
- **Arches**

These elements can be used, as appropriate, to make spatial arrangements that can define and articulate volumes and also provide the forms necessary to enable activities to take place as required by a building's function. In the early stages of the design process, these elements can be considered in simple diagrammatic form but, as the proposal is developed, their form, proportion, size, material, colour, texture and finish will be refined to achieve a more sophisticated outcome.

A simple composition of these elements in their most basic form can be explored in an almost infinite number of ways, by developing alternative expressions of the configuration and by exploring contrasts such as open versus closed, light versus heavy, and opaque versus transparent, as described on pages 128–31.

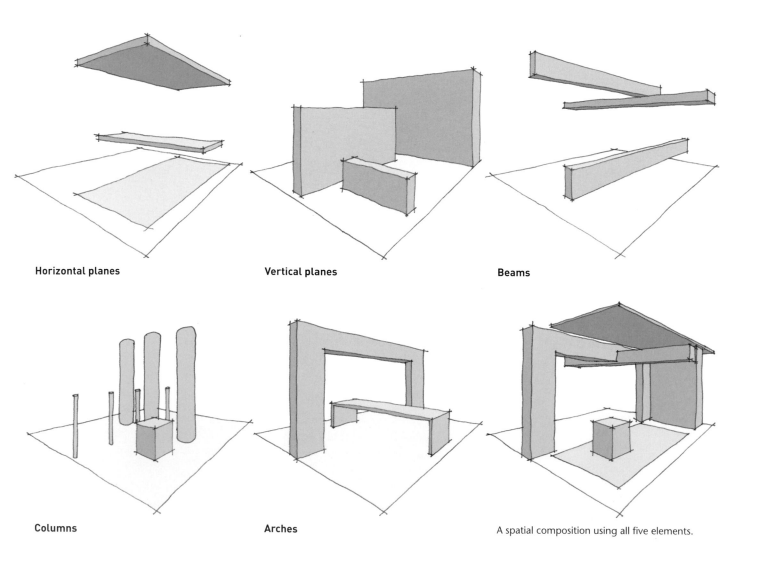

Horizontal planes

Vertical planes

Beams

Columns

Arches

A spatial composition using all five elements.

Right

Designed by Dake Wells
Architecture in 2011, the scheme
for Andy's Frozen Custard Home
Office in Springfield, Missouri,
USA is organized around an
irregular plane that has been
folded to create a rectilinear form
which becomes a composition of
horizontal and vertical elements.
This piece is placed in the
existing building as an insertion.
It contains spaces and defines
the 'leftover' spaces around it.
The red colour is a reference
to the client's trademark use
of cherries in their product.

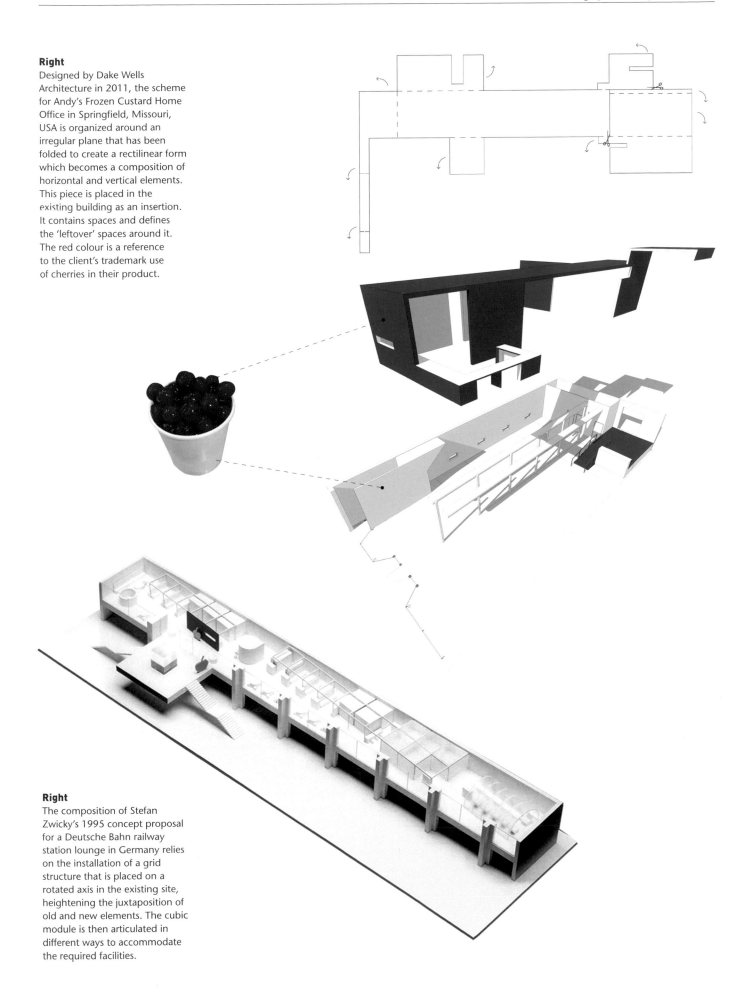

Right

The composition of Stefan
Zwicky's 1995 concept proposal
for a Deutsche Bahn railway
station lounge in Germany relies
on the installation of a grid
structure that is placed on a
rotated axis in the existing site,
heightening the juxtaposition of
old and new elements. The cubic
module is then articulated in
different ways to accommodate
the required facilities.

The studio of B Mes R 29 Arquitectes in Lleida, Spain provides a straightforward example of how a sketch plan can be developed into a three-dimensional composition. The planning arrangement consolidates all the support facilities (reception and waiting areas, toilet, kitchen, store) into a rectangular space in the middle of the site, leaving the surrounding space as a work zone. Together, the position of this rectangle and its relationship with the space within which it sits establishes the primary element of the spatial composition – a 'space within a space'. The two-dimensional rectangle can be considered as a three-dimensional 'box', and its definition and articulation become the key consideration in the development of the spatial composition.

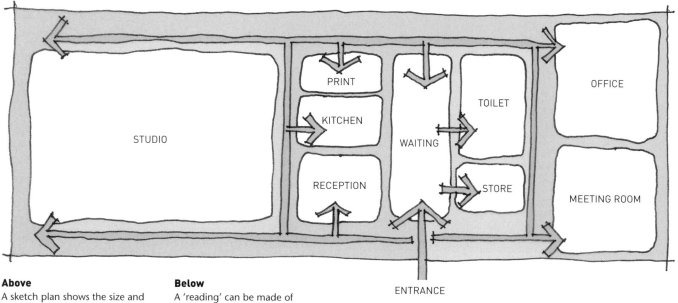

Above
A sketch plan shows the size and location of spaces in relation to the site, as well as the circulation routes connecting them. At this point, the major planning decisions have been made and do not need to be changed.

Below
A 'reading' can be made of the sketch plan to provide a two-dimensional composition of shapes. Here, the support facilities are grouped together and read as an orange rectangle, while the surrounding 'leftover' space becomes the work zone.

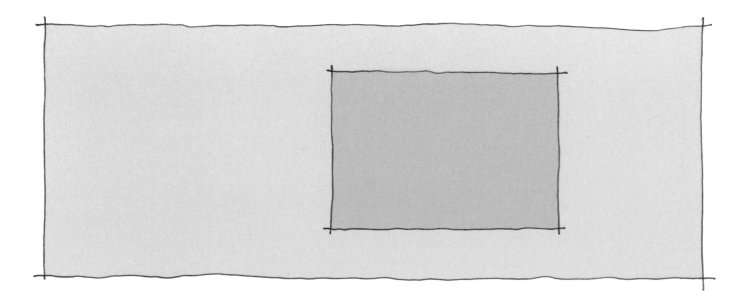

Above
Models and drawings can be used to develop a range of spatial compositions to explore the two-dimensional diagram – they will always relate in some way to decisions recorded in the sketch plan.

Below
Once a satisfactory spatial composition has been established its form can be transferred back to the sketch plan, which can now be developed into a more finished planning proposal. More and more detail (concerning dimensions, thicknesses, doors, furniture, fixtures and fittings) can be added as decisions are made and the scheme progresses.

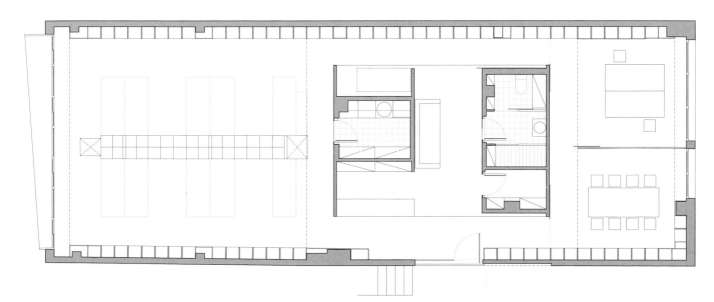

Left
Höweler + Yoon Architecture designed this scheme for the new headquarters of the Boston Society of Architects in 2013, in which a glossy bright green plane folds down from the upper level to become the staircase, before folding back up to become the ceiling. The spatial composition revolves around the insertion of this bold element, hanging in the existing building in Boston, USA.

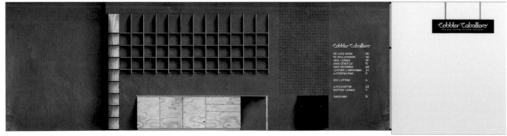

Section

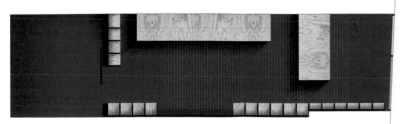

Plan

Left
Cobbler Caballero is a small shop in Sydney, Australia that specializes in the repair of shoes, watches and leather goods. The interior is defined by a composition of vertical planes that are articulated and proportioned in different ways to become shelving, work benches, counter, display and signage. Here a plan and section through the shop, designed by Stewart Hollenstein in 2011, show the precise placement of the scheme's components.

Case study Exploring contrasts

Cahier d'Exercices boutique, Montreal, Canada / Saucier + Perotte Architectes

Cahier d'Exercices is a boutique located on the ground floor of an historic building in Montreal. The design scheme, 2011, is a fine example of an interior's spatial composition being defined by a number of simple elements (horizontal planes, vertical planes, beams and columns) that set up a series of bold contrasts exploring many of the opportunities available to an interior designer. Old versus new, light versus heavy, black versus white, shiny versus matt, rough versus smooth and colour versus tone are all explored in this commercial retail environment.

Top right

A view from the entrance establishes the contrasts set up within the boutique. The opposing peripheral walls are old, dark and roughly textured to one side and new, light and smooth to the other. The slick, glossy ceiling contrasts with the matt floor and transforms itself from black to white, drawing people to the rear of the store, while the rails from which most of the garments hang are formed of a delicate, white-painted metal section, providing a lightness of touch. Finally, the existing cast-iron columns, picked out in primary red, set up another contrast between pure colour and the surrounding monochromatic environment.

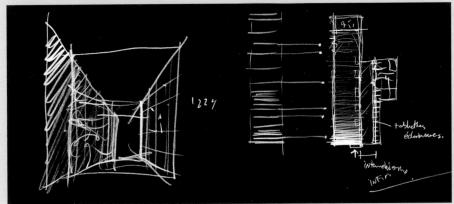

Right

These conceptual sketches show opportunities for contrasts being explored on both the section and the plan.

Right and far right

Strong contrasts are established between the 'heavy' existing wall (whose rough, random texture is painted dark grey) and the newly inserted 'lightweight' display wall, which has clean sharp lines and a white finish. The detailing of the wall promotes the idea that this element is floating free of the floor and ceiling.

STEP BY STEP EXPLORATORY MODEL MAKING

Model making is a crucial part of the interior design process and is especially important for inexperienced designers with less understanding of the potential a two-dimensional plan might have for translation into an exciting three-dimensional composition of space. When modelling from a plan, most people's instinctive reaction is to translate lines into walls using white card, but this can result in a rather uninspiring cellular spatial composition. For the interior designer, the interest lies in discovering new

ways to define and articulate space, and exploratory model making can be key to this endeavour. Allow yourself the freedom to make many models to explore the different ways in which a given plan could be articulated in three dimensions, then combine the most successful ideas to form new and better compositions that progress the proposal further.

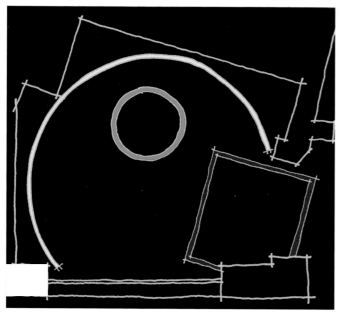

1 A diagrammatic plan can be analyzed to create a two-dimensional composition of key shapes and lines. This becomes the departure point for a series of models that explore potential three-dimensional configurations.

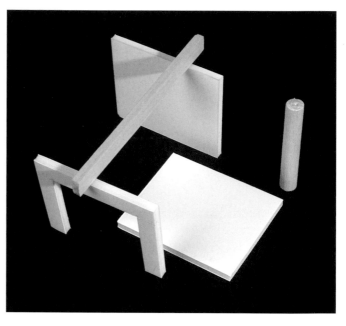

2 Columns, beams, arches, horizontal planes and vertical planes are elements used to define interior space. Try making your own components and then use them to articulate a two-dimensional composition in a variety of ways.

3 You can use a wide variety of materials to explore opacity, translucency, perforation, texture, colour, pattern and finish in your models.

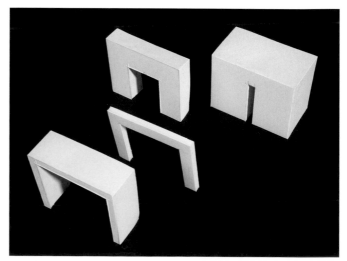

4 Experiment with material choice, size, thickness and texture in your exploratory models. Set up contrasts between different elements of the composition to investigate issues such as light versus heavy, opaque versus transparent and open versus closed. This image shows arches of varying thicknesses.

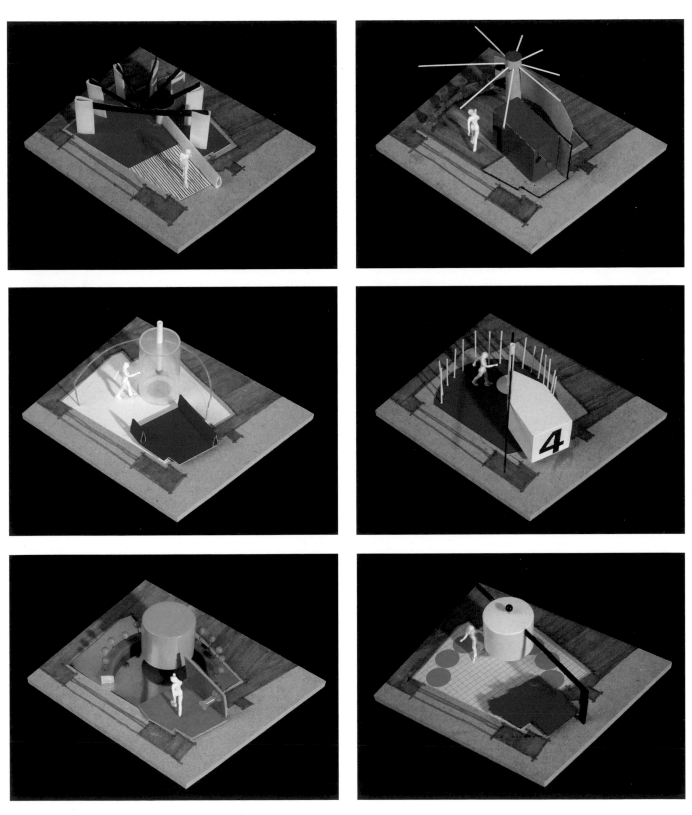

5 In this sequence, a selection of models explore the same two-dimensional composition (an identical plan was drawn on the base of each model) in a variety of ways to produce potential three-dimensional spatial compositions. The more investigations a designer undertakes at this stage, the better: they can combine interesting aspects of these models to create additional models that can further develop the proposal.

CHAPTER 8
DESIGNING IN SECTION

Introduction

Most interior designers will instinctively use the plan as the prime tool for developing a building's spatial organization and, while this is often an appropriate starting point, it is not always advisable. This approach can potentially lead to dull interior schemes that lack spatial interest, and most projects will benefit if the design of the section is considered in conjunction with the plan. Indeed, there are many situations where the spatial organization is all about the form of the section, and the plan is delivered as a consequence of decisions made in section.

When working in section, the designer can consider the three-dimensional form of the existing building. Some buildings will have an interesting volumetric composition that the designer should understand in order to make an appropriate response, while other buildings could be termed 'blank canvases', in which case the designer's task is to inject spatial interest into the volume by changing the profile of the section. This chapter will address the importance of the section in the development of the three-dimensional planning process.

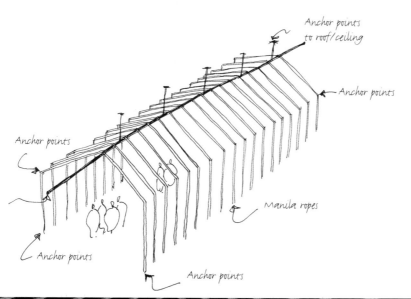

This page
An early concept sketch by Architects EAT shows how their 2008 scheme for Maedaya Sake & Grill, a Japanese restaurant in Victoria, Australia, was driven by the form of the section. A simple plan and nondescript site are given a clear identity by a profile designed to evoke the idea of a traditional Japanese house. The shape is articulated by a repeated element formed of ropes stretched in tension, a reference to traditional sake packaging.

Manipulating volumes

When considering the organization of the section (as opposed to the layout of the plan), the interior designer has an opportunity to alter the volumetric composition of a building. If sections of floors are removed and voids are created, it may be possible to connect different levels and the resulting contrast in heights can lead to dramatic spatial relationships in a building's interior. As well as being a means of exploring how vertical spatial connections can be established, working in section can also encourage the interior

designer to explore how horizontal connections can be made between different spaces on the same level.

When working within a single space, considering the section will allow the designer to modify the heights of different parts of that space, while also providing an opportunity to give thought to how the form and shape of the space can be modelled. In some cases, this will be in response to an existing building's profile (which might already have some articulation) or it might be done to give a rather bland empty shell some character.

Left
American architect Neil M. Denari often explores projects through the section. His 1996 proposal for an architecture and design gallery in Tokyo, Japan occupies a third-floor space in a typical urban block. A folded plane is inserted into the space, redefining the shape of the volume.

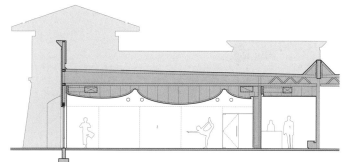

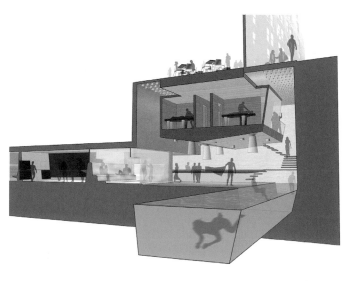

Above and above right
Yoga Deva occupies a building of little architectural merit in a commercial complex in Gilbert, Arizona, USA. In 2008, blank studio architecture remodelled this uninspiring space to create a yoga studio that facilitates meditation and contemplation. The designers introduced a profiled ceiling consisting of three cylindrical, inverted vaults running the length of the space. In addition to providing visual interest, the ceiling houses services and controls natural light and acoustics.

Right
In this 2007 proposal for Loftel, a hotel in New York, USA, Joel Sanders Architects created a subterranean leisure space by developing a complex section that brings three-dimensional articulation to a linear plan. Natural and artificial light is introduced through glass blocks set into the pavement and restaurant floor, while the outer profile of treatment rooms suspended in a double-height space creates a lowered ceiling above a swimming pool that has been excavated out of the ground below. Both vertical and horizontal connections of spaces are explored.

STEP BY STEP EXPLORING THE OPPORTUNITIES OFFERED BY THE SECTION

When working with an existing building, it is important to identify the opportunities it offers for the section to be modified. This can be done in a methodical manner that enables the designer to explore the site's potential quickly and clearly.

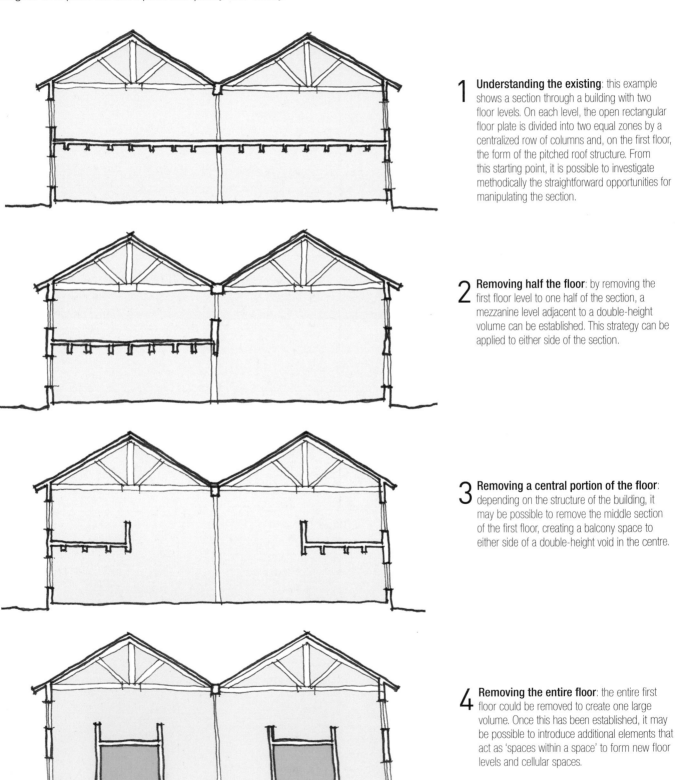

1 **Understanding the existing**: this example shows a section through a building with two floor levels. On each level, the open rectangular floor plate is divided into two equal zones by a centralized row of columns and, on the first floor, the form of the pitched roof structure. From this starting point, it is possible to investigate methodically the straightforward opportunities for manipulating the section.

2 **Removing half the floor**: by removing the first floor level to one half of the section, a mezzanine level adjacent to a double-height volume can be established. This strategy can be applied to either side of the section.

3 **Removing a central portion of the floor**: depending on the structure of the building, it may be possible to remove the middle section of the first floor, creating a balcony space to either side of a double-height void in the centre.

4 **Removing the entire floor**: the entire first floor could be removed to create one large volume. Once this has been established, it may be possible to introduce additional elements that act as 'spaces within a space' to form new floor levels and cellular spaces.

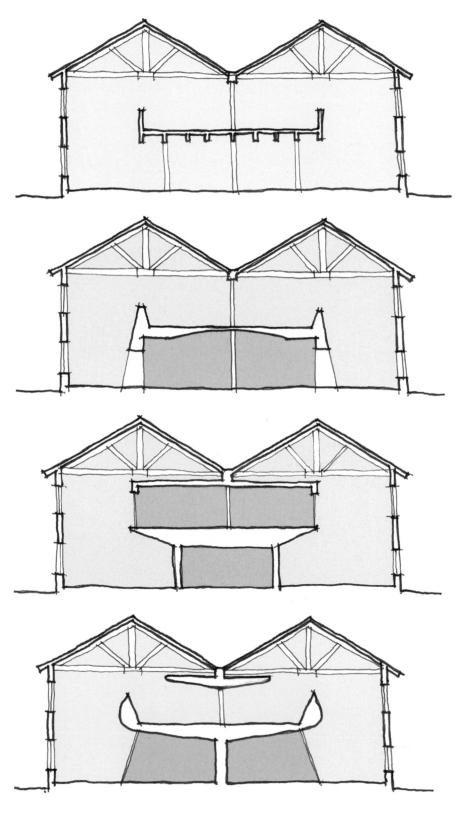

5 **Removing the perimeter sections of the floor**: the structure of the existing building may allow for sections of the first floor at the perimeter of the building to be removed, leaving a centralized mezzanine with visual connections to the ground floor below. If this strategy is deemed appropriate, then the interior designer can investigate countless ways in which the form of the section can be manipulated while delivering the principles of this configuration.

6 **Investigations of form (1)**: here, sloping columns support the central mezzanine level while a semi-enclosed space below it incorporates a vaulted ceiling. The forms of the new elements contrast with the existing building.

7 **Investigations of form (2)**: alternatively, the upper level could be conceived as a separate enclosed volume with its own ceiling and glazed walls (providing physical separation while maintaining some visual connections). At ground-floor level, the form of the underside of the first-floor level tapers in section to create more intimacy within the enclosed centralized space.

8 **Investigations of form (3)**: another approach could be to manipulate the shapes of volumes in the scheme in order to create appropriate spaces for the activities involved. The form of the spaces can be angled or curved as necessary – the section provides endless opportunities to introduce spatial drama to the proposal.

Case study Designing in section (1)

Canary Wharf Underground Station, London, UK / Foster + Partners

This Underground station was opened in 1999 as part of the Jubilee Line Extension to provide access to a new business district in London's Docklands and was planned so that it could become the city's busiest peak-time station. The building occupies a strip of land 300 metres (385 feet) long, with a glazed canopy at either end that draws people and light down on to the main concourse below. At ground level, there is a landscaped park between the entrances. The underground volume is sited on the hollow of the original West India Dock and the interior space is established through the use of 'cut-and-cover' techniques. The section of the interior has been sculpted to articulate the relatively simple plan. Essentially, the floors are narrow at the lower level and step out to become wider at the upper level. A simple, clear circulation strategy is established by the centralized positioning of the escalators and the placement of amenities to the perimeter of the main concourse. The section is profiled to provide voids to house services and incorporate maintenance gangways that enable repair work to be undertaken without obstructing passengers.

Above

The main concourse is a huge volume with cathedral-like qualities thanks to its vast scale and the arched form of the section.

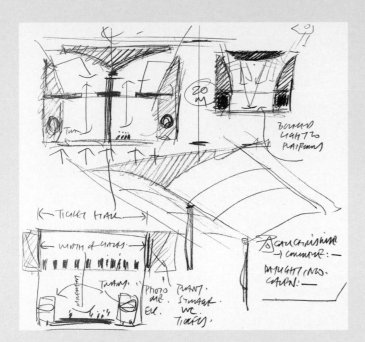

Left
Early sketch drawings show that the interior is formed from a repeated module that has been developed in section. Arched ribs spring from a central beam to create a vaulted roof structure.

Below
This drawing shows how the spatial arrangement of the interior is organized around the section. At platform level, a single central platform serves both train directions. Central escalators move passengers to and from the main concourse, where the centralized columns help to define 'in' and 'out' circulation routes. Services are pushed to the perimeter of the main concourse, keeping it clear of obstructions.

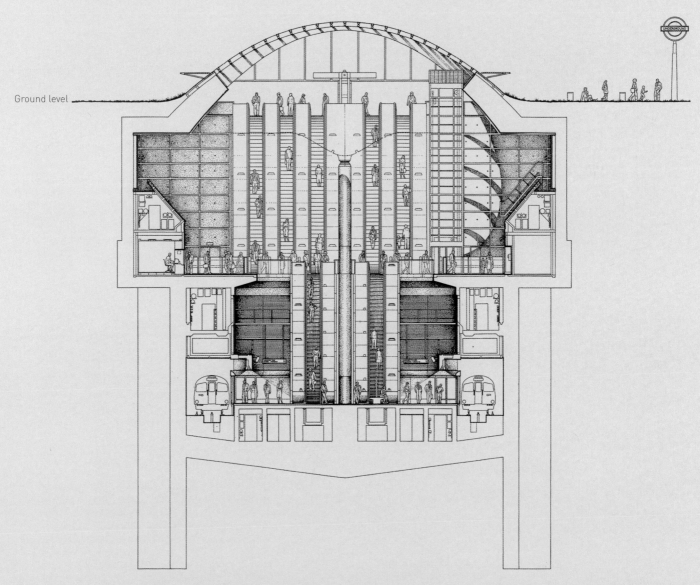

Ground level

Simple plans, complex sections

An interior can often have a very straightforward plan but its section will be a far more intricate and sophisticated arrangement of spaces and volumes. Le Corbusier's Unité d'Habitation in Marseille, France (1952) is one of the best examples of a building designed around its section, which is far more complex than the relatively simple plan.

From the outside, the Unité d'Habitation has the appearance of a typical seventeen-storey residential building. On plan, the main body of the building forms an elongated rectangle, approximately six times longer than it is wide, that is arranged on a north–south axis. A simple planning configuration is established with apartments arranged in a linear organization around a central 'interior street' that provides access to lifts (elevators) and stairs. There are 29 rectangular apartments to one side of the corridor, and lifts and stairs to the other, leaving space for 25 apartments on that side. While the plan of the building is simple and clear, the way in which the section has been organized provides interest and solves practical problems

in an ingenious way. Where one would expect a seventeen-storey building to have seventeen access corridors, there are only five (located on the second, fifth, ninth, twelfth and fifteenth floors). This is possible due to the way the section of the building is conceived as a module of three floors that is repeated five times. Each three-storey module contains two apartments, configured in section as an L-shaped volume consisting of two levels. These pairs of L-shaped apartments interlock around an internal street and, as a consequence, apartments to one side of the corridor are entered at their upper level while apartments on the other side of the access route are entered at their lower level. An additional two floors (inserted at levels seven and eight) house amenities including a bar, restaurant, shops, hotel and commercial offices.

The result of this clever manipulation of the section is that apartments benefit from a dual aspect, with east-facing spaces arranged to acknowledge the morning sun and west-facing spaces the afternoon sun.

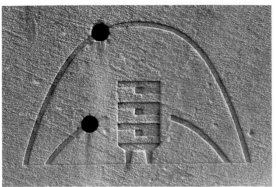

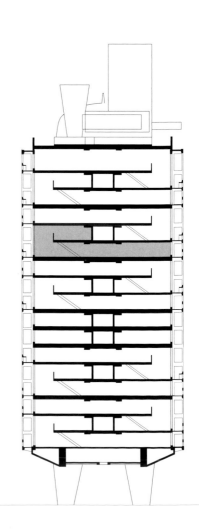

Left
The straightforward rectilinear exterior of Le Corbusier's Unité d'Habitation at Marseille belies the complexities of the section used to organize the interior.

Bottom left
A diagram cast into the concrete of the ground floor explains the principles of the section to users of the building, showing its orientation and the clever configuration of the apartments and access corridors. The higher and lower arcs indicate the path of the sun in summer and winter respectively.

Right
A diagrammatic section through the building shows pairs of L-shaped apartments interlocking around the internal street to form a three-storey module that is repeated five times, with amenities located on the seventh and eighth floors.

Case study Designing in section (2)

Proposed dental surgery / Sam Leist (Kingston University, UK)

This student project made a proposal for a private dental practice to be situated in the basement of a planned office development in central London, UK. The solution was driven by the section for two reasons, one conceptual and the other practical.

First, the designer developed a conceptual idea in response to making the observation that the ceiling assumes great importance for patients in dental surgeries, as their supine position during treatment focuses their attention on the overhead activity in the space. As a result, a proposal was developed in which the ceiling became a three-dimensional, modulated 'inverted landscape' and this necessitated investigation by section.

Second, the basement site had to be accessed from the street and so a key aspect of the scheme was concerned with establishing a ground-floor entrance and developing vertical circulation routes to the subterranean level where the practice was to be housed. As the context for the project was a new-build speculative office block, the designer was able to propose establishing a connection between the basement volume and the space allocated to retail on the ground floor. As a result, the design of the section was the prime consideration when developing the form of the connecting volume and the configuration of the staircase and lifts (elevators) within it.

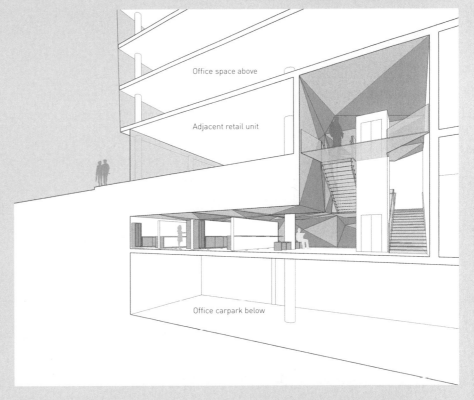

Above

A sectional perspective shows the turquoise ceiling to be the dominant element of the design proposal. Made up of triangular panels that are arranged into a series of interconnected irregular pyramid forms, the feature ceiling manipulates the volume of the otherwise bland basement space and controls the arrangement of the plan. This is achieved as a result of considering the proposal in section.

Below

A section drawn through the entrance and staircase shows the new volume created to connect the basement to the street. The basement ceiling folds up the wall of the void and then folds again to become an entrance canopy that projects out of the building, inviting people in. Visitors descend via the staircase or lift (elevator) and are deposited at the reception desk.

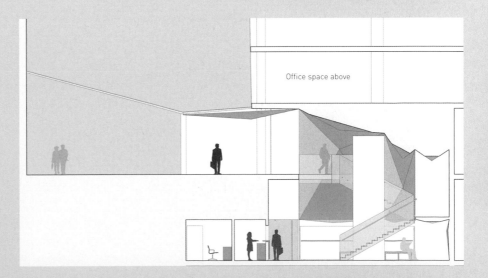

Responding to the existing site

The interior designer will often respond to an existing site by using the section as a means of introducing drama to an otherwise bland volume. In essence, the response involves either covering or adding to the existing. When an existing building presents a section that has some articulation and interest, the designer can make a response that takes advantage of the opportunities provided. This will generally involve developing an understanding of the site and the elements of the section that are of interest or importance. The building's immediate context or environment may be of significance and so developing an understanding of issues such as the following will be of value:

- **How does the building relate to adjacent buildings and/or the surrounding landscape?**
- **Are there important views or vistas that should be established or eliminated?**
- **How does the existing section respond to the building's orientation?**

Once the building's relationship with the external factors is understood, it is important for the interior to analyze the section in terms of its internal configuration. To this end, an appreciation of the following issues will be helpful:

- **How do the existing levels work within the building?**
- **Might the form of the existing section influence the response?**
- **Will existing elements (such as roof trusses, columns, beams and apertures) influence the design of the section?**
- **How will the building's structure affect any remodelling of the section?**

Having established an understanding of the context in which the work is to be undertaken, the interior designer might develop a proposal involving the manipulation of the section solely through the removal of parts of the existing building, through the introduction of new elements into the existing section or a combination of the two.

Below
This student project for a showroom for bathroom fittings is located in a railway arch at Vauxhall station in London, UK. A sectional drawing through the length of the arch establishes the relationship of the interior space with the adjacent streets and the railway tracks above.

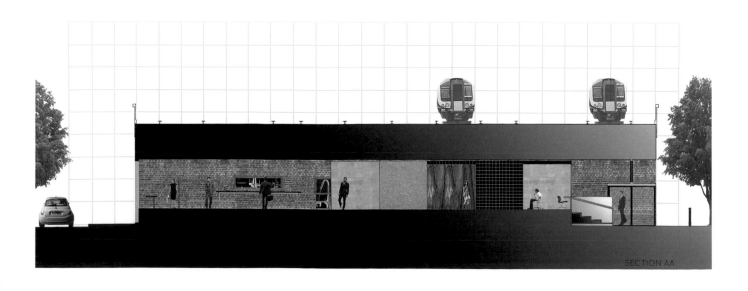

SECTION AA

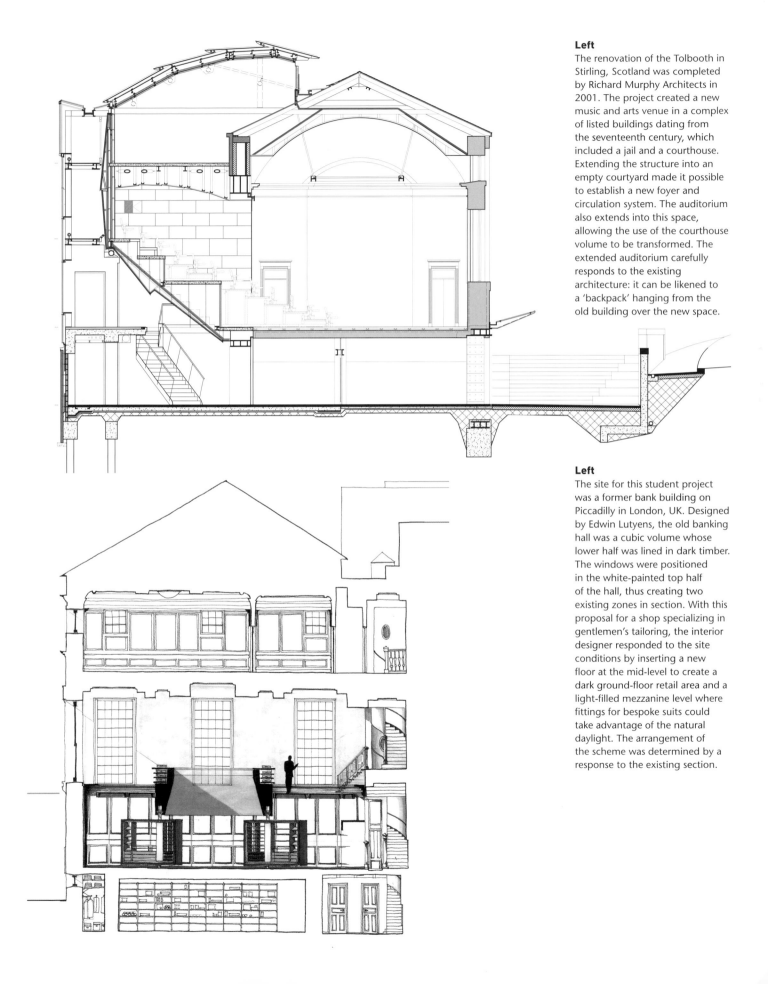

The renovation of the Tolbooth in Stirling, Scotland was completed by Richard Murphy Architects in 2001. The project created a new music and arts venue in a complex of listed buildings dating from the seventeenth century, which included a jail and a courthouse. Extending the structure into an empty courtyard made it possible to establish a new foyer and circulation system. The auditorium also extends into this space, allowing the use of the courthouse volume to be transformed. The extended auditorium carefully responds to the existing architecture: it can be likened to a 'backpack' hanging from the old building over the new space.

Left
The site for this student project was a former bank building on Piccadilly in London, UK. Designed by Edwin Lutyens, the old banking hall was a cubic volume whose lower half was lined in dark timber. The windows were positioned in the white-painted top half of the hall, thus creating two existing zones in section. With this proposal for a shop specializing in gentlemen's tailoring, the interior designer responded to the site conditions by inserting a new floor at the mid-level to create a dark ground-floor retail area and a light-filled mezzanine level where fittings for bespoke suits could take advantage of the natural daylight. The arrangement of the scheme was determined by a response to the existing section.

Sectional models

When considering the spatial organization of a building, there are two ways in which an interior designer can use sectional models: as part of the design process and as a presentation tool.

Used as a part of the design process, sectional models are an invaluable method of developing truly interesting three-dimensional proposals. A scheme can be quickly developed when the interior designer makes a number of simple sketch sections of the same portion of the proposal, forcing them to explore a number of options as to how this section could work. The more explorations they make, the more likely they are to achieve a satisfying result. This work can be tackled in different ways, depending on the conceptual approach to the project. If the designer is employing a strategy of 'insertion' or 'installation', then they might make a single model of a section through the existing building and place a number of explorations in it in order to test their impact. If a strategy of 'intervention' is planned, then the sectional models might be used to explore how the existing building fabric can accommodate additions and subtractions, requiring a number of

This page
Forming a crucial part of the design process, a student proposal for an airport duty-free shop is explored through a series of sectional sketch models, from an initial tentative start to a more developed study. The shape of the simple rectilinear volume is transformed and, as the scheme becomes more resolved, a greater amount of detail is investigated.

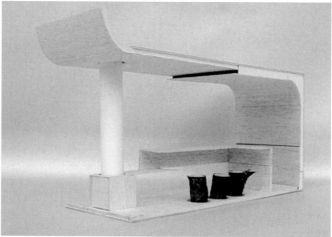

Far left
A student's sectional presentation model showing part of a scheme for a hairdressing salon manages to communicate the spatial relationship between the mezzanine and basement levels, as well as detail concerning the treatment of the building envelope.

Left
A sectional model through the whole building clearly shows the spatial arrangement of this student proposal for a restaurant.

Left
Made by a group of students to develop their understanding of the site on which they were working, this presentation model cuts a section through the existing building. When it was later shown in an exhibition, the model was arranged so that visitors could walk between the two parts.

models to be made. In this case, it is often easier to make the section as a long 'extrusion' that can then be sliced into smaller sections, speeding up the process.

Sectional models can also be used as a presentation tool to communicate the finished design proposal in a clear and effective manner. A model presenting a sectional view of a space can enable the viewer to appreciate the shape and form of the volumes that have been created, as well as providing them with an opportunity to place the new interior in the context of the host structure and its location. The model illustrates the relationship the interior has with the existing building and its surroundings.

For the model to be truly effective, it is best to present it so that the eye level of the viewer corresponds with that of a scale figure in the model. This helps the viewer to engage with the interior space and encourages the feeling that they are 'inhabiting' it.

CHAPTER 9
COMMUNICATING SPATIAL ORGANIZATIONS

Introduction

Interior designers prepare material to communicate their design intentions for a number of different reasons, and there are many methods they can use to do so. One determining factor will be the stage the project is at. At the start of a project, the designer might need to establish an understanding of the site and/or the building programme. In the middle of the process, it might be important for them to communicate a conceptual idea and the major design proposals, while at the end of the project complex information about detail will be required. In addition, an interior designer will have to communicate with many different people, who will have different levels of expertise and understanding. Drawings might be produced during an informal discussion with a colleague, to communicate ideas at internal team meetings in a design practice, to enable professionals from related design disciplines to understand a proposal or to present material to peers, such as the judging panel for a competition. More commonly, interior designers prepare material in order to present proposals to clients or to the general public, neither of whom might be able to read a design drawing.

The status of the material being presented will also have a bearing on the means of communication employed. During the early stages of a project, the proposal is more open and the task might be to present a variety of ideas that will inevitably be rather unresolved. At this point, it is important to present them in a loose manner that allows discussions to take place – there is always a danger in presenting very polished, formal drawings too early in the process. Once a scheme has been developed and the principles approved, there will be opportunities to produce finished material as appropriate.

As a general rule of thumb, it is best to start the communication process with bold, simple pieces of information that, once understood and agreed, can be developed into more complex, detailed material. The key to successfully communicating interior design work is to ensure that the method of communication used is appropriate for the stage of the project, the qualities of the scheme in question and the audience for whom the material is being prepared. This chapter will identify some of the formats interior designers can use to help communicate the spatial organization of buildings.

Right
This 2012 diagram of the Tate Modern Gallery in London, UK was designed by Cartlidge Levene and Studio Myerscough to assist visitors with way-finding. As its aim is to provide the general public with a clear understanding of how the building works, this diagram has a lot to teach the interior designer in terms of effective communication of volumetric configurations. The diagram has to explain a complex arrangement of spaces and vertical circulation: it uses a sectional view, colour, symbols and words to ensure the information is more easily understood.

Useful drawing types

Interior designers have a variety of different drawing types at their disposal that they can use to communicate a scheme. The most common forms are:

- **Diagrams**
- **Plans**
- **Sections**
- **Axonometric drawings**
- **Perspective drawings**

All these drawing types can be important in their own right, but the exact nature of the project (the form of the site and the decisions that have been made in terms of its development) will determine which drawing types are appropriate at any given time. While a plan is generally an essential part of the communication process, on some occasions a single three-dimensional drawing such as an axonometric can illustrate a scheme with ease.

When preparing a presentation, there is a danger that the designer will produce a series of drawings without sufficient thought and only afterwards consider what needs to be communicated about the scheme. A more intelligent approach would be for the designer to analyze the proposal at the start of the process, establish which aspects are important and require explanation and then produce the appropriate material to support the verbal presentation of the project. This will often lead to a clearer presentation that requires much less preparatory work.

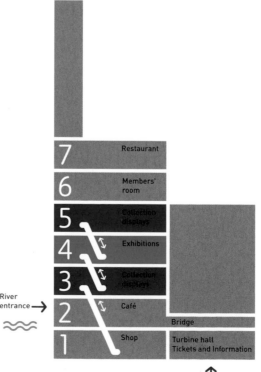

River entrance →

7 Restaurant
6 Members' room
5 Collection displays
4 Exhibitions
3 Collection displays
2 Café
1 Shop

Bridge
Turbine hall
Tickets and Information

Main entrance ↑

Diagrams

To some extent all interior design drawings are diagrams – an abstract representation of the proposed built reality. In this context, the term 'diagram' is used to describe how abstraction can allow complex ideas and relationships to be communicated simply and clearly through graphic representation.

The spatial configuration of a building is often complicated and difficult to understand. Interior designers use diagrams in order to simplify information, so that fundamental principles can be easily conveyed. These diagrams can portray information using imagery; they might be two-dimensional or three-dimensional, portraying the essence of a scheme through the use of axonometric or perspective formats. Diagrams will typically rely on both images and text, although it could be argued that a diagram is more successful if it can communicate clearly without words.

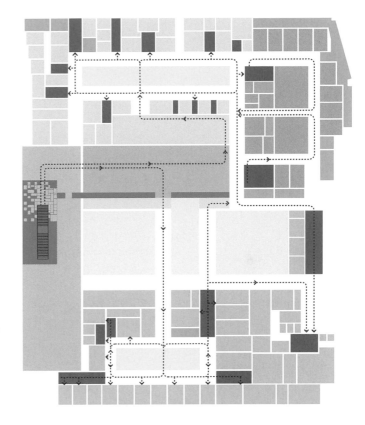

Below
Thin Office is a shared workspace in Singapore that accommodates an IT company and a multimedia company. The interior was designed by Studio SKLIM in 2010, and this diagram uses an axonometric format to explain the strategy behind the spatial organization.

Right
Colour is used to group spaces into zones and identify different circulation routes in an attempt to clarify the complex planning of the Kangbuk Samsung Hospital in Seoul, Korea, designed by Hyunjoon Yoo Architects in 2010.

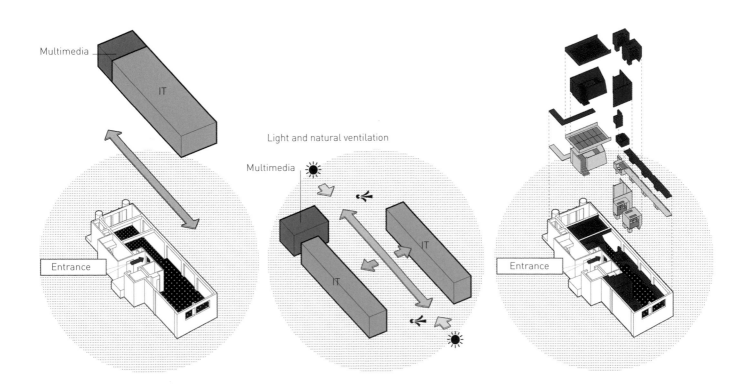

Plans

Floor plans are used to communicate information about the horizontal relationship of interior spaces. Plans are two-dimensional measured drawings that are created by taking a horizontal section through a building (or design proposal) and recording everything that is located below that level. Typically the section is cut about 1 metre (3 feet) above floor level. Floor plans are one type of orthographic projection used by designers and it is important that they are drawn using the correct line weights as well as the appropriate conventions to communicate building elements such as doors, windows and staircases.

Most of the interior designer's spatial organization work is drawn either to a scale of 1:100 (or 1/8" = 1'-0") or at 1:50 (or 1/4" = 1'-0"). For very diagrammatic work, the designer might employ a scale of 1:200 (or 1/16" = 1'-0"), but the small size of this scale hardly allows them to undertake any meaningful interior design work. As schemes are developed, work will move up to a scale of 1:20 (or 3/4" = 1'-0"), allowing the designer to resolve

much more detail. The amount of information shown on plan drawings will depend on the stage of the project, the purpose of the drawing and the nature of the scheme. Early in the design process, drawings may be quite sketchy and only communicate the way in which spaces relate to each other. As a scheme develops, much more information will be added concerning the exact size and shape of elements, furniture arrangements, floor patterns and materials.

Floor plans can be simple line drawings that communicate factual information about the scheme, or the interior designer can use shadow projection and colour to provide greater understanding of the mood and character of the scheme. If a building has a number of levels, the designer will draw a plan of each floor. When these are drawn on the same sheet, it is usual for them to be arranged in the same orientation, with the lower floor plan at the bottom and subsequent plans arranged in order above.

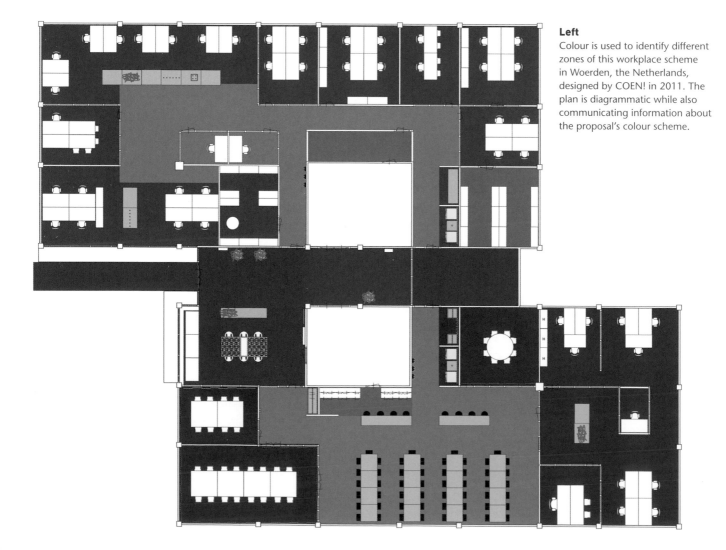

Left
Colour is used to identify different zones of this workplace scheme in Woerden, the Netherlands, designed by COEN! in 2011. The plan is diagrammatic while also communicating information about the proposal's colour scheme.

Right
Simple line drawings by Robert Gurney show the planning arrangement of this remodelled house in Washington DC, USA (2011). The floor plans are arranged for ease of understanding, with the lower level at the bottom, entry level in the middle and the upper level at the top.

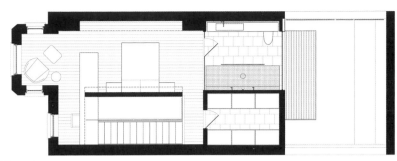

Upper level floor plan

Entry level floor plan

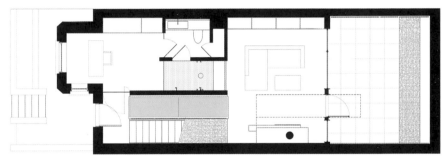

Lower level floor plan

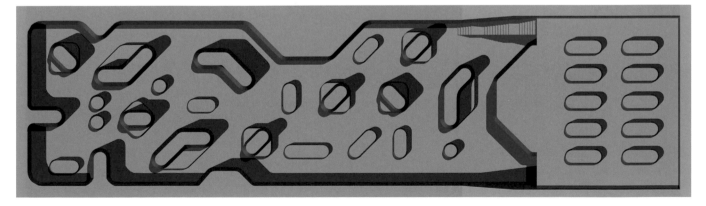

Bottom
Clients can often find it impossible to read floor plans, but shadow projection gives this 2007 Gameworld exhibition layout for the Laboral Art Centre in Gijon, Spain by Leeser Architecture some three-dimensional articulation to help understanding and increase interest.

Sections

Sections are used to communicate information about the vertical relationships between spaces in an interior design proposal. A sectional drawing will generally convey two aspects of the proposal: the profile of the volume concerned and the treatment of the interior elevations contained within the section. These two-dimensional measured drawings are created by taking a vertical slice through a building and recording everything located beyond the line of the cut. When deciding where the section is taken, the designer must ensure that the appropriate elements of the scheme are communicated. Like plans, sections are a type of orthographic projection used by interior designers and it is important that they are also drawn using the correct line weights and conventions.

Only basic interior design information can be communicated at a scale of 1:100 (or 1/8" = 1'-0") and most interior design schemes will benefit from being drawn at scales of 1:50 (or 1/4" = 1'-0") and 1:20 (or 3/4" = 1'-0"). As with plan drawings, scales will increase as the design process progresses, as larger scales allow more detail to be shown.

Section drawings can be simple line drawings, but these can prove difficult for the untrained viewer to read. Greater understanding can be achieved by showing the plan and section together, and by rendering the elevations of the interior (in the section) to show more detail of the spaces concerned.

Below
This 1778 drawing by Sir John Soane of the Pantheon in Rome, Italy illustrates how a section can provide information about the volumetric profile of the interior (identified here in pink) and the detail of its elevation. In this instance, the detail and the shadow projection help explain the curved floor plan and domed roof form.

Left
A freehand section drawing is a valuable design tool and can also be used to present complicated information in a user-friendly manner, as shown by this drawing explaining the use of daylight and natural ventilation in the National Assembly for Wales by Rogers Stirk Harbour + Partners in Cardiff, UK (2005).

Below
The conceptual Mix House designed by Joel Sanders in 2004 proposes a scheme whereby apertures capture sounds from the surrounding environment, allowing the user to create ambient soundscapes in the interior. Here a section drawing is used as a diagram to explain the principles of the scheme.

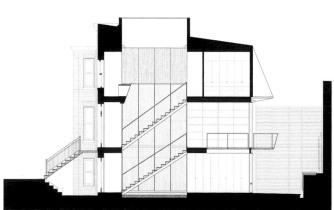

Below
Simple line drawings by Robert Gurney Architect show the existing (left) and proposed (right) sections through this remodelled house in Washington DC, USA (2011). The proposed section provides information about the elevation of the interior spaces, showing panel sizes, their arrangement and relationship to the new roof light.

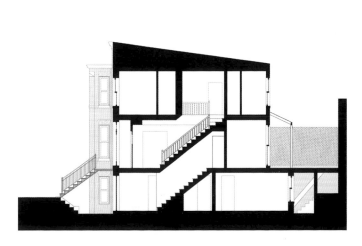

Axonometric drawings

It can be difficult for those unfamiliar with the conventions of design drawing to read plans and sections. This is primarily because these drawing types record only a part of the information about the three-dimensional space they represent. Plans and sections will only tell the full story when read in conjunction with each other. Axonometric drawings help to bridge the gap between a two-dimensional and a three-dimensional representation of an interior, as they combine plan and section to show a two-dimensional view of space that has a three-dimensional quality. Because an axonometric view is one that can never be perceived in reality it has practical limitations, but its strengths as a diagrammatic means of communication can make it a powerful means of explaining a building's spatial composition.

Axonometric drawings are a great way of providing an overview of the scheme's spatial composition, showing large and complex buildings as a totality. Different elements in a configuration can be separated in an exploded axonometric drawing in order to foster greater understanding of the spatial relationships that have been established, while still maintaining a sense of how the composition works as a whole. An exploded axonometric can allow a ceiling to be 'lifted' out of the drawing so that the rest of the interior can be clearly seen.

As with all drawing types, the quality of line used will depend on the circumstances – freehand or sketch axonometric drawings can be useful tools in the early stages of a project.

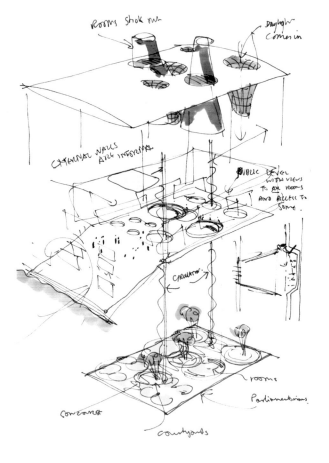

Left
An early concept sketch by Rogers Stirk Harbour + Partners uses an exploded axonometric projection to explore the design principles of the National Assembly for Wales, Cardiff, UK (2005).

Below
For this exploded axonometric drawing explaining the scheme for their own studio in Missouri, USA, Dake Wells Architecture used simple black lines to show the existing site and blocks of colour to highlight the newly installed elements (2007).

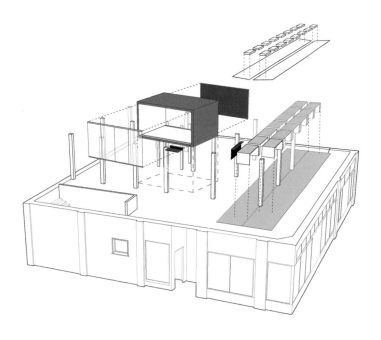

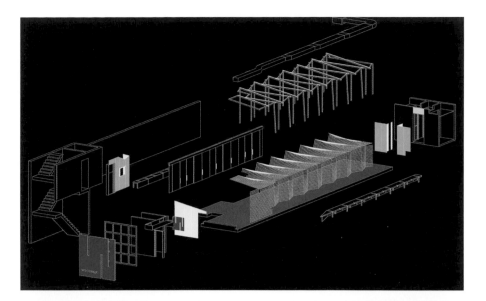

Left

Woodwalk is a showroom in Delhi, India designed to promote timber as an interior finish. This 2010 exploded axonometric drawing by Vir.Mueller Architects identifies the component parts of the interior as individual elements that come together to form the completed scheme.

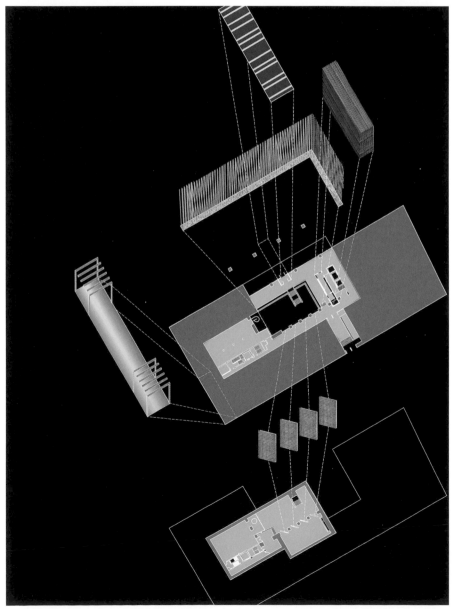

Left

The Blatz is a mixed-use complex housed in the former Blatz Brewery building in Milwaukee, USA. In 2007, Johnsen Schmaling Architects remodelled the public circulation spaces and this exploded axonometric drawing shows the scheme as a collection of independent insertions that are placed in response to the restrictions of the existing building. Simple block colour is used to code each element.

Perspective drawings

Perspectives are perhaps the easiest drawings for the untrained eye to understand as they offer a realistic three-dimensional view of a design scheme. Interior designers generally use perspective views to create visuals of interior spaces, but this convention can also provide a highly effective means of communicating an overview of the scheme's spatial organization.

Because perspective views combine information about a scheme's plan and section, they were traditionally far more difficult to produce than straightforward orthographic drawings. Computer drawing software has made it relatively easy to produce complicated

perspective compositions that can be manipulated to provide highly informative presentation material, which can often explain a building's organization in a single image. Exploded perspectives allow component parts of a scheme (such as different floor levels) to be separated for a greater understanding of the whole, while sectional perspectives allow the existing building to be cut through, revealing the interior spaces.

As with all interior design drawing types, there is an opportunity to formally construct perspective drawings either by hand or by using computer software and then tracing off freehand presentation material.

Left
This sectional perspective drawing of Joel Sanders Architects' proposal for the Loftel hotel in New York, USA (2007) manages to communicate a lot of complicated information concerning the spatial relationships in the scheme, while also providing a flavour of the interior's mood and character. The drawing type helps the viewer to easily understand the proposal.

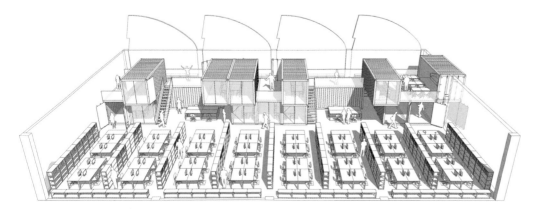

Left
Architectural practice group8 named the project to design their own workspace Cargo, as the scheme involved placing used shipping containers in a former industrial space near Geneva, Switzerland (2010). To facilitate this perspective view of the whole interior, the roof and front wall of the building are removed. The line drawing of the rear wall enables the viewer to understand the profile of the roof structure. Shadow projection enhances the three-dimensional qualities of the drawing.

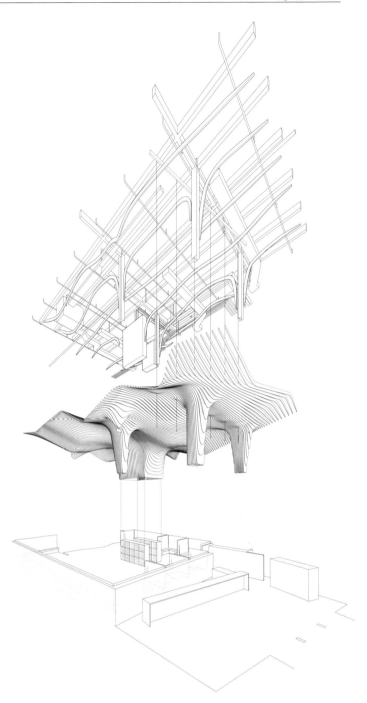

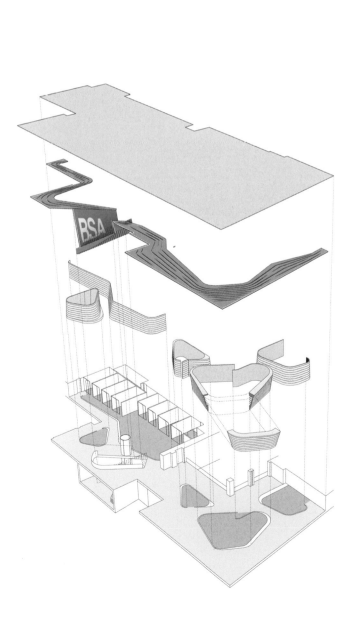

Left

This proposal by Höweler + Yoon Architecture for the Boston Society of Architects' new headquarters, 2013, uses a bold exploded-perspective format as a diagrammatic means of communicating the different layers of the scheme. Curved partitions and a folded soffit/staircase element are sandwiched between the existing floor and ceiling.

Above

The Banq restaurant in Boston, USA was conceived in 2008 NADAAA (formerly Office dA) as a scheme in two parts, consisting of a flexible floor level (where furniture can be moved and relocated) and a fixed ceiling, the striated wood slats of which conceal services and are also 'dripped' and 'slumped' to clad columns. This exploded perspective emphasizes this idea by separating the two elements above and below the eye level, which is highlighted by the horizontal line., 2008.

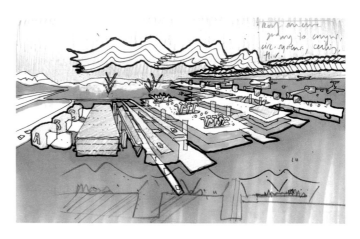

Above
NFOE et Associés Architectes used a perspective-plan view to communicate the layout of their scheme for the OVO fertility clinic in Montreal, Canada (2009). Colour and shadow projection help the perspective to clearly explain the complex plan.

Below
This computer-generated perspective of Joel Sanders Architect's 2003 scheme for the Charles Worthington hair salon in New York, USA offers an overview of the building envelope (showing the arrangement of the support facilities) and then lifts out the main salon area to provide a view of the interior that communicates the quality of the space.

Above
This freehand perspective sketch illustrates the big conceptual idea behind the spatial arrangement of the Madrid-Barajas airport in Spain, designed by Rogers Stirk Harbour + Partners in 2006. The lively, confident line quality promotes understanding of a complex scheme.

Below
Here an exploded perspective is used as a diagram to explain the 'kit of parts' used by De Leon & Primmer Architecture Workshop to organize the visitor centre of the Yew Dell Botanical Gardens in Kentucky, USA (2010).

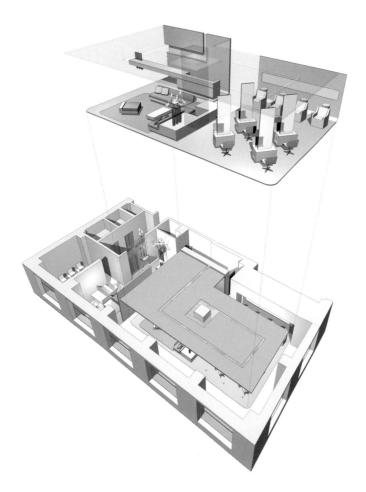

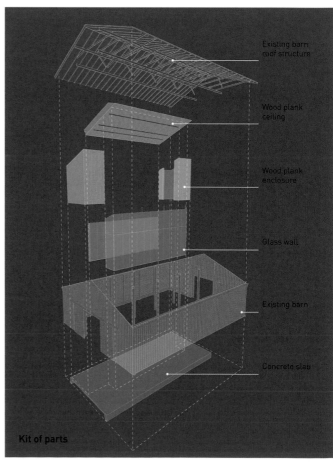

Existing barn roof structure

Wood plank ceiling

Wood plank enclosure

Glass wall

Existing barn

Concrete slab

Kit of parts

Case Study Communicating a Spatial Concept

Hair salon proposal / Oliver Corrin (Kingston University, UK)

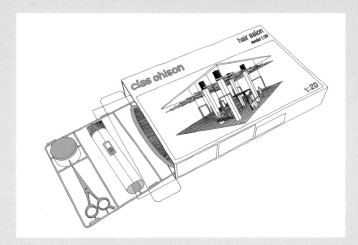

The first drawing establishes the fundamental spatial concept for the scheme: a 'kit of parts' to be assembled on site, presented as a toy-model construction kit emerging from its packaging.

The second drawing shows the 'model kit' in the process of assembly, explaining the design process as well as the concept underpinning the scheme. The drawing of the designer's workspace adds a playful touch to the narrative.

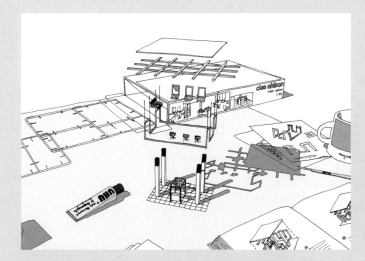

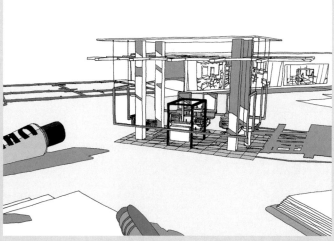

The third drawing in the sequence shows the kit of parts coming together to form the final composition of elements – each element of the whole is clearly identifiable before it is brought together with the others.

A perspective drawing of the workspace shows a 'model' of the finished proposal. When read in conjunction with the earlier diagrams it is easy to understand the spatial ideas that have been employed to establish the composition.

This project proposed a small hair salon within a department store. The scheme was conceived as a collection of lightweight linear components with dimensions that were determined by the grid of the existing interior (itself determined by the dimensions of the existing ceiling, columns and floor tiles). The new components were designed as a kit of pre-manufactured parts that could be assembled on site and which woud have minimal contact with the existing interior. The concept is communicated clearly through a series of playful perspective drawings that animate the process from its starting point through to the finished proposal. Simple sketch drawings that provide a step-by-step journey through the design process can provide valuable support to a verbal presentation.

Freehand/sketch drawings

Hand-drawn sketches are essential design tools as they allow designers to explore and develop ideas, and interior designers therefore often use them to establish options for solving a particular problem. In a design practice, many conversations will be had around sketch drawings and these are often the best way of communicating with colleagues. A good, simple sketch will usually communicate an idea far more successfully than any number of spoken words.

While happy to use freehand drawings in the studio, many designers will adopt a more polished drawing style when presenting work to clients. In many cases this is entirely appropriate, but there are also plenty of occasions when sketch drawings can be a far more successful presentation tool. Sketch drawings have the advantage of being less formal and more accessible (clients will often delight in the skill evident in a freehand drawing) and, as the line quality is less precise than that of a ruled or computer-generated drawing, the material becomes slightly more ambiguous. This can be highly advantageous in the early stages of a design project, when the scheme is less than fully resolved and is presented in order for a discussion to take place as to how it might develop.

Hand-drawn sketches will be used to create simple diagrams at the start of the design process, but the interior designer should not overlook the option of using this approach to present highly detailed drawings of complex schemes. Computer software or physical models will often be produced to generate material that the designer can then use to quickly trace off some freehand drawings.

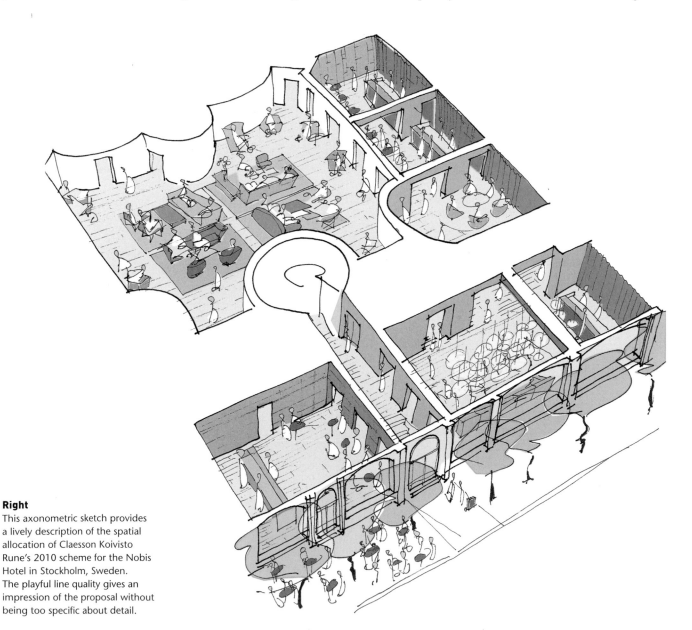

Right
This axonometric sketch provides a lively description of the spatial allocation of Claesson Koivisto Rune's 2010 scheme for the Nobis Hotel in Stockholm, Sweden. The playful line quality gives an impression of the proposal without being too specific about detail.

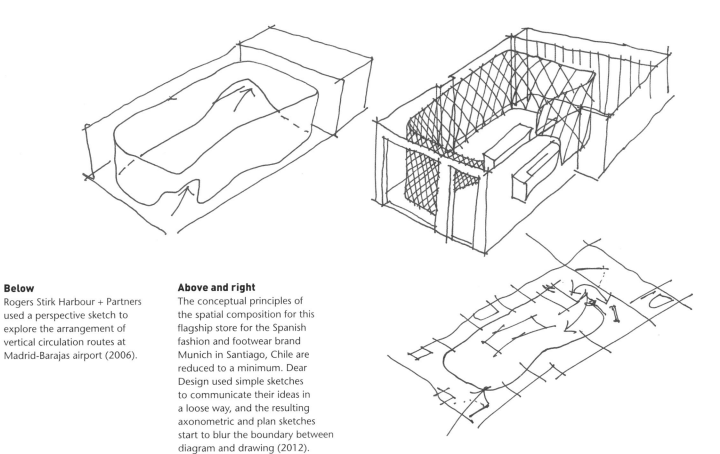

Below
Rogers Stirk Harbour + Partners used a perspective sketch to explore the arrangement of vertical circulation routes at Madrid-Barajas airport (2006).

Above and right
The conceptual principles of the spatial composition for this flagship store for the Spanish fashion and footwear brand Munich in Santiago, Chile are reduced to a minimum. Dear Design used simple sketches to communicate their ideas in a loose way, and the resulting axonometric and plan sketches start to blur the boundary between diagram and drawing (2012).

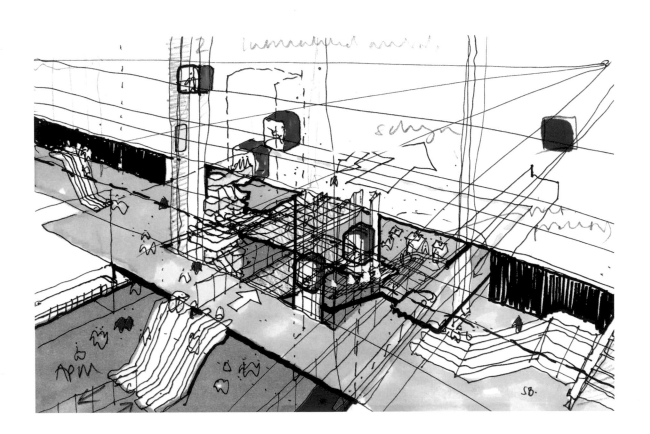

STEP BY STEP CREATING FREEHAND DRAWINGS

While some designers have a natural ability to draw beautifully by hand, most will need to develop this skill. The following material can help anybody produce better freehand drawings, but the key to gaining confidence is practice. There really is no substitute for this: professional designers draw every day, producing a wealth of material, and become more and more accomplished as a result. Ultimately, there are no short cuts.

1 Select the right materials to work with – pens need to be capable of laying down a line quickly and it is helpful to have a selection of line weights to hand. Paper should be lightweight and thin enough to facilitate tracing (for example tracing paper, layout paper or detail paper).

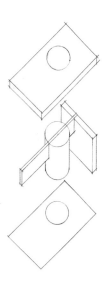

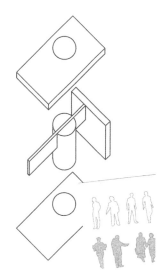

2 Use a drawing board or computer software to formally create the 'bones' of the drawing – these figures will act as 'underlays' for the freehand drawing. A sheet of underlay figures can be printed out and used again and again.

3 Using the underlay material, trace off drawings and figures. The tracing process will usually involve using many layers to develop the drawing and add more detail. Don't be precious about your drawings: if one goes wrong, simply start another. It can take lots of attempts to get it right.

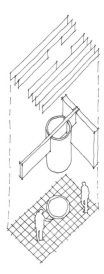

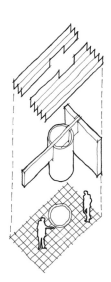

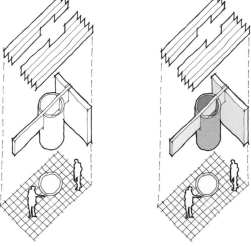

4 Use the thinnest pen to construct your drawings, allowing the lines to cross confidently at corners (this allows you to draw quickly, with a fluid line quality). Add thicker lines afterwards for emphasis.

5 The finished drawing might be black and white or you can add colour as appropriate, either by hand or with the help of computer software.

Models

Many clients find it impossible to understand design drawings but can easily appreciate – and be delighted by – a model of a scheme. As models are time-consuming (and therefore expensive) to produce, it is important, in the first instance, to clarify whether a model is necessary and, if so, what it will be used for. All too often a designer will have an ambition to make a model that is too detailed for its purpose and invariably shows far more of the scheme than is necessary. If the designer considers the issues described below at the outset, they will need less time to communicate their ideas more successfully and can avoid the temptation to create a 'doll's house' model.

Models are made for many reasons: as a tool for the designer to understand and develop the design of the scheme, to serve as three-dimensional diagrams to explain the components of a scheme to colleagues or to present the finished scheme to the client. Early exploratory models can be quite crude and produced quickly using scrap materials, while a presentation model may take weeks to construct, using quality materials in order to achieve a highly crafted finish. The purpose of the model should be established before work commences to ensure an appropriate outcome is achieved as economically as possible. Once the purpose of the model has been established, decisions can be made as to the following:

- **At what scale should the model be made?**
- **From what materials should the model be made?**
- **How much of the scheme is it necessary to make?**
- **How will you see inside the building to view the interior?**
- **Is the model to be diagrammatic or will it communicate the colour and quality of materials used in the scheme?**

Right
A simple diagrammatic model shows the conceptual idea for the organization of this house in Valencia, Spain designed by Fran Silvestre Arquitectos in 2010. The model aids communication by showing only the key components of the spatial composition.

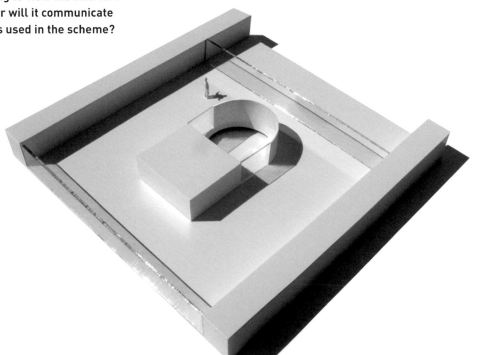

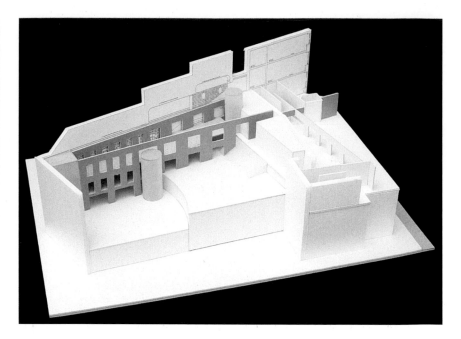

Above
Early in the design process, models can be used to explore the spatial composition of a scheme. Here void/solid, opacity/transparency and different materials are investigated in a student project to create an HIV clinic.

Above
Once the design of a scheme has been established, the principles of its organization can be explained in quite diagrammatic form. This student project proposed a nightclub in a former cinema building, and a 1:100 (approximately 1/8" = 1'-0") scale model uses colour to clearly explain the key elements of the new spatial composition. The existing building is suggested by sectional drawings cut to the form of the site's profile.

For interior designers, one of the most challenging aspects of model making is ensuring that the viewer has an appropriate view of the interior. To this end, models are often made without a ceiling but this solution can be unsatisfactory as the ceiling is often an essential component of an interior space. Sectional models offer a great way of establishing the qualities of an interior space while also allowing the viewer to appreciate the proposal. On larger projects, a sectional model will also make it possible to explain relationships between a number of different volumes.

A model can be a useful means of communicating the relationship between the existing site and the new interior. Designers will often implement a strategy to clarify what exists and what is new: this might involve using one material (or finish) for the existing and another for the new elements, or it might mean using a neutral colour such as white, beige or grey for the existing and introducing the new interior in full colour or through a single contrasting material, such as wood or acrylic.

It is important to remember that models, like drawings, can be used to communicate different aspects of a design scheme, from the conceptual ideas behind the spatial proposal to the precise detail found in a finished presentation model. To communicate well, the interior designer must know when to use which approach – often a series of models that become increasingly detailed will allow understanding to develop through the design process.

Below
The scheme for Las Arenas (2011) remodelled a bullring in Barcelona to create a contemporary leisure and entertainment complex. This sectional presentation model has been carefully considered to communicate information about the relationship of the new structure designed by Rogers Stirk Harbour + Partners to the existing building, showing how it acts as an insertion that is independent from the masonry wall that defined the circular plan of the original arena.

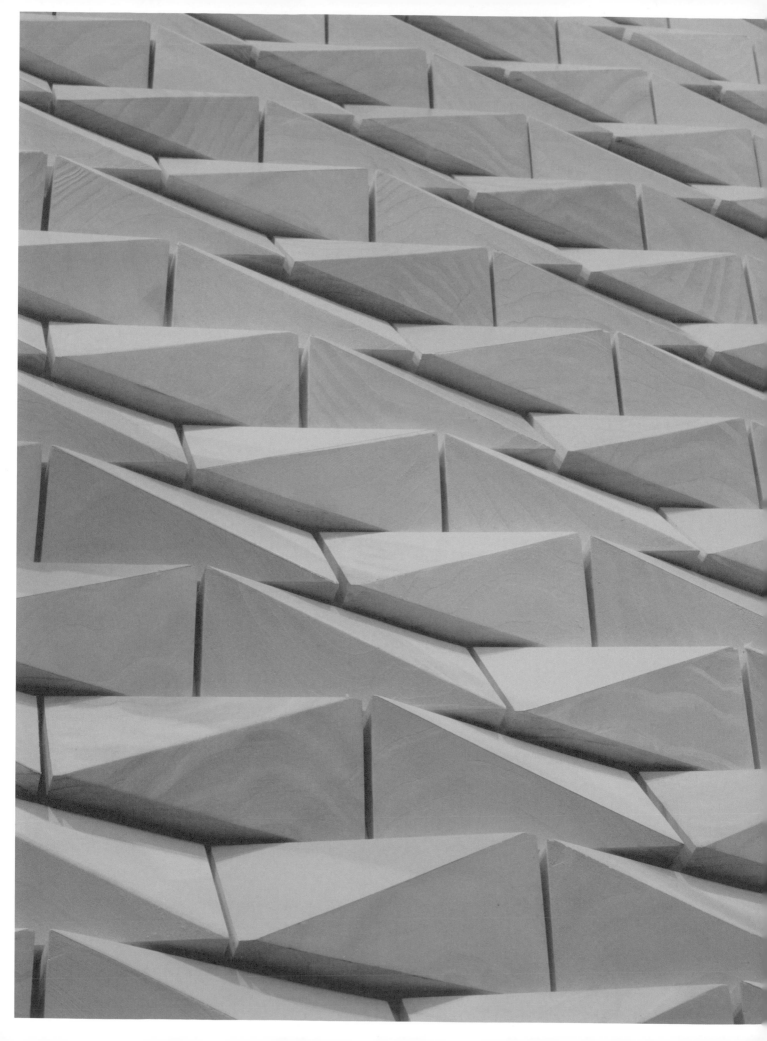

CHAPTER 10
WHAT NEXT?

Introduction

Although resolving the spatial organization of an interior proposal is a major aspect of the design process, it is only a part of the project's journey from inception to completion. Interior design is rarely a simple linear process and each project will progress along a slightly different route towards its realization. The exact course may depend on the size and complexity of the project, the designer's approach and other external factors such as timescale and budget. Although design practices will have different ways of approaching a project, they will usually identify key stages of the design process to clarify their method for both themselves and the client. Interior design projects will typically include the following phases:

- **Research**
- **Ideas/concepts**
- **Development**
- **Detailed design**
- **Realization**

Architectural projects are generally structured in a more formal way that is prescribed by local professional legislation. In the UK, the Royal Institute of British Architects (RIBA) has this responsibility. In 2013, RIBA proposed that its Plan of Work (originally introduced in 1963) should be simplified to the following stages:

- **Preparation**
- **Concept design**
- **Developed design**
- **Technical design**
- **Specialist design**
- **Construction**
- **Use and aftercare**

The scale and scope of most architectural projects is larger and more complex than most interior design work and so these projects demand a more defined process. There are, however, clear parallels between the unregulated approach of commercial interior design companies and the regulated architectural profession. Whether a project is developed in an architectural or an interior design context, it is likely that the spatial organization, or space-planning, aspect of the work will take place around the concept/design development stages of the process. The ensuing work will include:

- **The development of the planning in detail**
- **The detailed design of elements of the scheme**
- **The consideration of materials and finishes**
- **The specification of furniture and equipment**

Below
With offices in London and Dubai, Kinnersley Kent Design is an international design practice that specializes in retail and leisure design. This diagram explains the five-stage design process the practice employs: research, design concept, design development, design detail and implementation. The spatial organization of a scheme usually occurs during stages two and three of this process.

Detailed planning

The development of a scheme's spatial organization forms the skeleton of the planning arrangement: once this has been established, it is possible to flesh out the proposal by progressing some of the detail. This will involve recognizing which activities will take place in each space and providing for their needs – the interior designer will consider the precise arrangement, form and size of elements as well as their material, colour and texture. This work is usually be undertaken at ever-increasing scales (1:20 or 3/4" = 1'-0" scale) and larger) and, as more is understood about the scheme, decisions made at this stage may prompt the re-evaluation of some earlier planning decisions as well as informing the detailed design work to come.

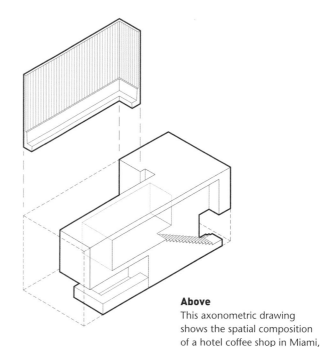

Above
This axonometric drawing shows the spatial composition of a hotel coffee shop in Miami, USA designed in 2008 by NC-office. At this point in the process, the necessary spaces are defined but are yet to be articulated in any detail.

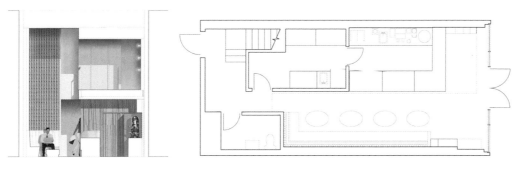

Left and far left
The plan and section are developed in more detail, enabling decisions to be made about the specific planning of the staircase, the doorways, the furniture layout and the toilet. Information concerning the module sizes of the counter units and the wall cladding is included and will inform the detailed design work to come.

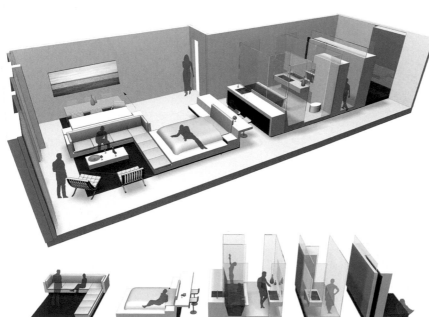

Left
Joel Sanders Architects' 2007 scheme for the Loftel in New York, USA proposed a hotel that captures the essence of loft living. On such a large and complex project, the spatial organization might establish the size, shape and location of each room, while the next stage of the process concerns the development of the detailed planning of each particular space. In this case, a series of modules was developed to address precise functional requirements, such as seating, sleeping, washing and storage. These modules could be arranged in various configurations to suit the size and shape of each situation, from small studios to luxurious suites.

STEP BY STEP THE DESIGN PROCESS

Working in the retail and leisure fields, London-based practice Kinnersley Kent Design use a five-stage process to develop interior design proposals. Here, different phases of this work are illustrated using a project for a department store in Abu Dhabi as an example.

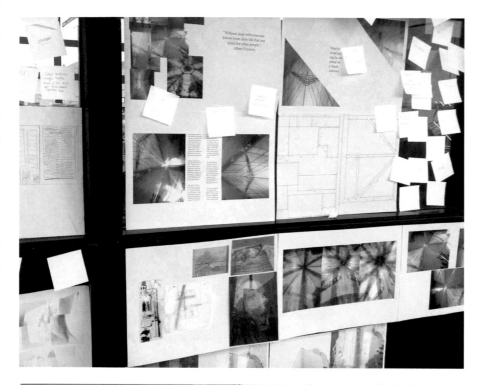

1 Research: most projects start with a period of research. The exact nature of this work will depend on the job, but it is likely to involve developing an understanding of the client, the building programme and the site. The interior designers will undertake precedent studies to learn how others have approached similar situations.

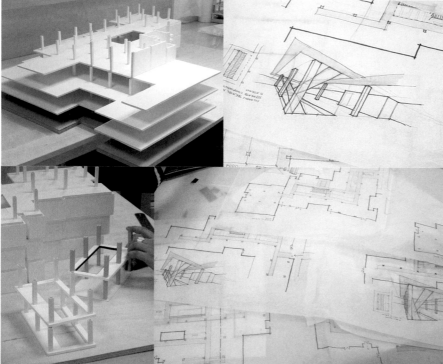

2 Design concept: the initial research undertaken will inform understanding of the problem at hand and lead to the development of the big ideas that will drive the scheme forward. The bones of the spatial strategy may be developed at this point.

Glossary

analogy
A comparison between things that have similar features, often used to help explain a principle or an idea.

aperture
An opening formed in the fabric of a building (can be in a floor, wall, roof, etc.).

Bauhaus
A German art and design school that operated from 1919 to 1933 and which was famous for an approach to design and design education that combined crafts and the fine arts.

brief
A set of instructions or information that defines the scope or requirements of a project.

cellular
As used in this book, a composition that is made of small parts.

conservation
The protection of structures and buildings, especially from the damaging effects of human activity.

cut-and-cover
A simple method of construction for shallow tunnels where a trench is excavated and roofed over with an overhead support system strong enough to carry the load of what is to be built above the tunnel.

extrusion
A shape formed by pushing a material through a profiled opening.

facade
The front elevation of a building.

mezzanine
A small extra floor between one floor of a building and the floor above.

Modernism
A philosophical movement that arose from wide-scale and far-reaching transformations in Western society in the late nineteenth and early twentieth centuries. Modernism, in general, includes the activities and creations of those who felt the traditional forms of art, architecture, literature, religious faith, philosophy, social organization and activities of daily life were becoming outdated in the new economic, social and political environment of an emerging, fully industrialized world.

modular
One of a set of separate parts that, when combined, form a complete whole.

narrative
A story or a description of a series of events.

orthographic drawing
A means of accurately recording a three-dimensional object through a set of two-dimensional drawings (typically plans, elevations and sections). The word is derived from the Greek *orthos* (straight) and *graphē* (drawing).

***plan libre* (free plan)**
A term originated by Le Corbusier to describe the 'free planning' made possible by post-and-beam construction, which enabled walls to be liberated from their structural role and to be used solely to define and divide space.

precedent
An action, situation, or decision that has already happened and can be used as a reason why a similar action or decision should be performed or taken.

refurbishment
To make a building look new again.

renovation
To repair and improve a building.

restoration
The act or process of returning a building to its earlier good condition.

strategy
A detailed plan for achieving success in situations such as the design of a building's interior.

tactic
A planned way of doing something.

topography
The physical appearance of the natural features of an area of land, especially the shape of its surface.

vernacular
A local style in which ordinary houses are built.

Further reading

Anderson, R., *The Great Court and the British Museum*, The British Museum Press, London, 2000

Brooker, G., *Key Interiors Since 1900*, Laurence King, London, 2013

Brooker, G. and S.Stone, *Re-readings: Interior Architecture and the Design Principles of Remodelling Existing Buildings*, RIBA Publishing, London, 2004

Brooker, G. and S.Stone, *Form & Structure*, AVA, Lausanne, 2007

Brooker, G. and S.Stone, *What is Interior Design?*, Rotovision, Hove, 2010

Brooker, G. and S.Stone, *Elements / Objects*, AVA, Lausanne, 2010

Campanario, G., *The Art of Urban Sketching*, Quarry Books, Beverly, 2012

Carter, P., *Mies van der Rohe at Work*, Phaidon, London, 1999

Ching, F., *Architecture: Form, Space and Order*, Van Nostrand Reinhold, New York, 2007, 3rd ed.

Coles, J. and N. House, *The Fundamentals of Interior Architecture*, AVA, Lausanne, 2007

Davies, C., *Key Houses of the Twentieth Century: Plans sections and Elevations*, Laurence King, London, 2006

Dunn, N., *Architectural Modelmaking*, Laurence King, London, 2010

Elam, K., *Geometry of Design*, Princetown Architectural Press, New York, 2001

Farrelly, L., *Representational Techniques*, AVA, Lausanne, 2008

Frampton, K., *Modern Architecture: A Critical History*, Thames & Hudson, London 1992, 3rd ed.

Frampton, K., *Le Corbusier: Architect of the Twentieth Century*, Harry N. Abrams, Inc., New York, 2002

Frampton, K. and D. Larkin, *American Masterworks: The Twentieth Century House*, Thames & Hudson, London, 2002

Hannah, G., *Elements of Design: Rowena Reed Kostellow and the Structure of Visual Relationships*, Princetown Architectural Press, New York, 2002

Hopkins, O., *Reading Architecture: A Visual Lexicon*, Laurence King, London, 2012

Hudson, J., *Interior Architecture: From Brief to Build*, Laurence King, London, 2010

Lambert, P., *Building Seagram*, Yale University Press, New Haven and London, 2013

Laseau, P., *Graphic Thinking for Architects and Designers*, John Wiley & Sons, Chichester, 2001

Leborg, C., *Visual Grammar*, Princetown Architectural Press, New York, 2006

Lidwell, W., K. Holden and J. Butler, *Universal Principles of Design*, Rockport, Gloucester, 2003

Littlefield, D. and S. Lewis, *Architectural Voices: Listening to Old Buildings*, John Wiley & Sons, Chichester, 2007

McCandless, D., *Information is Beautiful*, William Collins, London, 2012

Moryades, A. and A. Morris, *John Pawson: Themes and Projects*, Phaidon, London, 2002.

O'Kelly, E. and C. Dean, *Conversions*, Laurence King, London, 2007

Panero, J. and M. Zelnik, *Human Dimension and Interior Space*, Whitney, New York, 1979

Pile, J., *A History of Interior Design*, Laurence King, London, 2000

Plunkett, D., *Drawing for Interior Design*, Laurence King, London, 2009

Schittich, C., *Building in Existing Fabric: Refurbishment, Extension, New Design*, Birkhauser, Basel, 2004

Schittich, C., *Exhibitions and Displays*, Birkhauser, Basel, 2009

Schittich, C., *Work Environments*, Birkhauser, Basel, 2011

Schittich, C., *Interior Space*, Birkhauser, Basel, 2000

Schittich, C., *Interior Spaces: Space Light Materials*, Birkhauser, Basel, 2002

Scott, F., *On Altering Architecture*, Routledge, London and New York, 2008

Spankie, R., *Drawing out the Interior*, AVA, Lausanne, 2009

Stanton, A. and P. Williams, *Stanton Williams: Volume*, Black Dog Publishing Ltd, London, 2009

Sudjic, D., *John Pawson: Works*, Phaidon, London, 2000

Sutherland, M., *Modelmaking: A Basic Guide*, W. W. Norton & Co., New York, 1999

Index

Picture credits

T Top, B Bottom, C Centre, L Left, R Right
Any images not listed were supplied by the author.

COVER i29 interior architects; **1** Courtesy Dake Wells Architecture, principals: Andrew Wells FAIA and Brandon Dake, AIA; project team: Josh Harrold, Emily Harrold, John Whitaker; **3** Stefan Zwicky in collaboration with Trix and Robert Hausmann and Hans Jacob Hurlimann; **6** Matt Smith, Nottingham Trent University; **7T** © FLC/ADAGP, Paris and DACS, London 2014; **7B** © DACS 2014, courtesy Museum of Modern Art (MoMA), New York, © Photo SCALA, Florence; **8T** © DACS 2014, courtesy Museum of Modern Art (MoMA), New York, © Photo SCALA, Florence; **8BL** © DACS 2014; **8BR** Courtesy of Selldorf Architects; **10** Courtesy Estudio Nômada, Photography by Héctor Santos-Díes/BIS Images; **12–13B** Courtesy group8, photograph © Régis Golay, FEDERAL Studio, Geneva; **13TL** Archiplan Studio, Architects: Diego Cisi and Stefano Gorni Siluestrini; Photographer: Martina Mambrin; **13TR** Courtesy Casper Mueller Kneer Architects; **14–15 (all)** Courtesy HUA Li / TAO (Trace Architecture Office), Design Team: HUA Li, Guo Pengyu, Zhu Zhiyuan, Jiang Nan, Li Guofa; Photographer: Shu He; **16** Courtesy Jump Studios, Photographer: Gareth Gardner; **17TL** Apple Inc; **17CL** 1000Words/Shutterstock; **17CR** plo3/Shutterstock; **17B** US Patent and Trademark Office; **18TL, TC, TR** By permission of DAKS Simpson Group PLC; **18B** Alex Nevedomskis, Kingston University, London; **19T** Courtesy Kolchi Takada Architects; **19BL, 19BR** Courtesy Andrés Remy Arquitectos, design team and construction management: Guido Piaggio, Lilian Kandus; collaborators: Martin Dellatorre, Diego Siddi; photo: Alejandro Peral; **20T** Courtesy Integrated Field Co., Ltd., Photography Ketsiree Wongwan; **20C, B** Courtesy Estudio Nômada, Photography by Héctor Santos-Díes/BIS Images; **21 (all)** form-ula, Photography by Amy Barkow | Barkow Photo www.barkowphoto.com; **22** courtesy Fondazione Bisazza, Vicenza; **24T** © DACS 2014, courtesy Museum of Modern Art (MoMA), New York, © Photo SCALA, Florence; **24C, B** Courtesy Rogers Stirk Harbour + Partners, Photographer: Eamonn O'Mahony; **25T** © Richard Bryant; **25B** © Norman Foster; **26TL** © Ian Higgins; **26TR** © Nigel Young / Foster + Partners; **26B** Steve Greaves, www.stevegreaves.com; **27TL** Collection Het Nieuwe Instituut, Rotterdam. Archive code DOES, inv nr 001; **27TR** Stefan Zwicky; **27B** i29 interior architects; **28B** M Highsmith's America, Library of Congress, Prints and Photographs Division; **29T** courtesy Fondazione Bisazza, Vicenza; **29B** Courtesy Vector Architects, photo: Shu He; **30L** Christian Kerber/laif; **30R** Konstantin Grcic Industrial Design; **31T** © Norman Foster; **31B** with kind permission of the Natural History Museum, London and Imagination; **32T** Courtesy Ikea UK & Ireland; **32B** Courtesy JPD Total Retail Solutions, concept www.tiger-stores.com; visualizations, shop layout, furniture: www.jpd.lv; **33L** Photographer Robert Damora © Damora Archive; **33R** Yale University Art Gallery, New Haven (CT) © Photo SCALA, Florence; **34** Gareth Payne, Nottingham Trent University; **36** © 6a Architects; **37L** Gualtiero Boffi/Shutterstock; **37R** Tatjana Jakowicka, Kingston University, London; **38 (all)** Dan Brunn Architecture, Photography: Brandon Shigeta and Dan Brunn; **39T** Vladimir Radutny and Paul Tebben of SIDE architecture; **39BL, 39BR** Courtesy Dake

Wells Architects, design principal: Andrew Wells, FAIA, project architect: Mark Wheeler, AIA; photography Gayle Babcock, Architectural Imageworks, LLC; **40** Gareth Payne, Nottingham Trent University; **40 (all)** Gareth Payne, Nottingham Trent University; **41 (all)** x architekten; **42T** Stephen Crawley, Nottingham Trent University; **42B** Courtesy Hania Stambuk; **43 (all)** group8, photograph © Régis Golay, FEDERAL Studio, Geneva; **44T** h20 architectes; **44B** ///byn; **45TL, TR, BR** Courtesy Stanley Saitowitz | Natoma Architects Inc.; **45BL** TAGSTOCK1/Shutterstock; **46** i29 interior architects; **50L** Courtesy Coussée & Goris; **50R** © Ian Higgins; **51T** Groosman Partners; **51B** Image courtesy of Brooks + Scarpa Architects; **52** RUFproject & Nike Global Football Brand Design, photographer: Julian Abrams; **53 (all)** i29 interior architects; **54 (all)** The Architectural Archives, University of Pennsylvania, by the gift of Robert Venturi and Denise Scott Brown; **55 (all)** © Nigel Young / Foster + Partners; **59T** Crown Limited, courtesy of Bates Smart Architects; **59B** Virgin Atlantic Airlines in-house design team in collaboration with Pengelly Design; Nik Lusardi, lead designer of Virgin Atlantic's New Upper Class Suite, VAA; photo taken by Chris Lane; **60TL** Playtime dir. Jacques Tati © Rex Features Ltd; **60R** Kaory Tomozawa, Kohei Nashiguchi / Nikken Space Design Ltd.; **60BL** Eva Jiricna Architects Limited & A.I. Design s.r.o., Photo: Richard Davies; **61** courtesy Imagination; **62** Lam-Watson, O. (2013). Villa La Rotunda Ground Floor Plan, *Palladian Revival, Architectural Portfolio; Level One.*; **63T** courtesy PearsonLloyd, Project design: Tom Lloyd, Luke Parson, Sandra Chung, Tomohiko Sato, Marc Sapetti; **63B** courtesy Gwenael Nicolas, Curiosity; **65BR** courtesy RaichdelRio, estudi d'arquitectura; **66TL** © Ian Higgins; **66TR** Carlos Caetano/Shutterstock; **66CR, BR** Courtesy Zecc architects, photography by 'Jaroslaw', info@JRimageworks.com; **67TL, 67TR** © Groves Natcheva Architects Ltd; **67B** Akitoishii/Wikipedia; **68T** Margherita Spiluttini; **68C** Architekt Krischanitz; **68B** courtesy Kunsthalle Wien. Photo: Gerhard Koller; **70T, C** Courtesy Phi Design and Architecture, architect: Bill MacMahon, interior architect: Rebecca Cavanagh, photographer: Eric Sierins; **70BL, BR** © Ian Higgins; **71 (all)** courtesy Architekt Krischanitz ZT GmbH, photos: Lukas Roth; **72 (all)** Russell & George, photography by Diana Snape - www.dianasnape.co.au; **73T** Bates Smart, photography by Martin van der Wal; **73BL, BR** Courtesy Alex Cochrane, photography © Andrew Meredith; **74–75 (all)** Ippolito Fleitz Group GmbH, photography: Zooey Braun; **76–77 (all)** Collaboration between NC Design & Architecture Ltd (NCDA) and Laboratory for Explorative Architecture & Design Ltd (LEAD), photography: Dennis Lo Designs Ltd; **78** Courtesy Blacksheep, photography: Francesca Yorke; **80** Studio SKLIM; **81T** Courtesy Blacksheep, photography: Francesca Yorke; **81B** Courtesy YO! Sushi, photography: Paul Winch-Furness; **82L** Ippolito Fleitz Group GmbH, photography: Zooey Braun; **82R** Joyce Lai/flickr; **88–89 (all)** William Russell, Pentagram Design; **92, 93** Spacesmith, LLP; **94B, 95 (all)** courtesy B Mes R 29 Arquitectes SLP, direction: Xavier F Rodriguez i Padilla, Josep M Burgues i Solanes, collaborating architects: Arnau Ricart Real, Xavier Romero Monio, Cristina Cruz Gomez, photos: Amaneceres Fotograficos; **96–97 (all)** courtesy Ab Rogers Design, photographs © John Short; **98** Courtesy DAP Studio, photographer: Barbara Corsico; **100 (all)** Paulien Bremmer Architects in collaboration with Office Jarrik Ouburg; **101–104 (all)** Courtesy Orms; **105** Photographer: Miguel de Guzmán | www.imagensubliminal.com; **106 (all)** Courtesy DAP Studio, photographer: Barbara Corsico; **107 (all)** Courtesy Alan Chu & Cristiano Kato, photos: Djan Chu; **108L** Stanton Williams; **108R** © Peter Cook / View Pictures; **109TL** © Richard Glover / VIEW; **109TR** Richard Davies; **109B** © Richard Glover / VIEW; **110–111 (all)** Zecc Architecten, www.zecc.nl; Studio Rolf, www.rolf.fr; photos: Frank Hanswijk; **112** Gareth Payne, Nottingham Trent University; **113 (all)** Stanton Williams; **114–115 (all)** Alex Cochrane Architects, photography © Andrew Meridith; **116** courtesy Hania Stambuk; **117L** Courtesy Gundry & Ducker Architecture, Photographer Joe Clark; **117R** © Ian Higgins; **118–119 (all)** © Ian Higgins; **120** Courtesy Gwenael Nicolas, Curiosity; **122TR** i29 interior architects; **122L** Paul Warchol; **122BR** Courtesy Breathe Architecture, design and project architects: Linda Valentic & Jeremy McLeod; **124T** Paul Rocheleau; **125T** Courtesy Garcia Tamjidi Architecture Design, photo: Joe Fletcher Photography; **125B** Courtesy Gwenael Nicolas, Curiosity; **126T** Courtesy jones | haydu, contractor: Buck O'Neill Builders, Inc., photo: Bruce Damonte; **126B** Chris Gascoigne/VIEW Pictures/Alamy; **127 (all)** Courtesy Reinhardt-Jung, Frankfurt am main/Sydney, www.reinhardtjung.de, carpenter: Radix, Berlin, www.radix.de, photos: Lumen-Joppich u. Dorr GbR. www.lumenphoto.de; **128L** Courtesy Dear Design (Design team: Ignasi Llauradó, Eric Dufourd, Photo: Pol Cucala); **128R** Saucier + Perrotte architectes, photography: Marc Cramer and Gilles Saucier; **129T** Courtesy group8 architecture & urban planning: Laurent Ammeter, Adrien Besson, Tarramo Broennimann, Oscar Frisk, Manuel Der Hagopian, François de Marignac, Christophe Pidoux, Grégoire Du Pasquier; photograph: NOI pictures, Sébastien Löffler; **129B** Courtesy Gwenael Nicolas, Curiosity; **130TL** Courtesy Vector Architects, photo: Shu He; **130TR** Courtesy MSR (Meyer, Scherer & Rockcastle, Ltd), collaborating architects: Boutlinghouse Simpson Gates Architects, photo: Lara Swimmer; **130B** © Richard Glover / VIEW; **131T** dRMM, Photography: Alex de Rijke and Michael Mack; **131B** Paul Warchol; **133T** Courtesy Dake Wells Architecture, principals: Andrew Wells FAIA and Brandon Dake, AIA; project team: Josh Harrold, Emily Harrold, John Whitaker; **133B** Stefan Zwicky in collaboration with Trix and Robert Hausmann and Hans Jacob Hurlimann; **135 (all)** Courtesy B Mes R 29 Arquitectes SLP. Direction: Xavier F Rodriguez i Padilla, Josep M Burgues i Solanes. Collaborating architects: Arnau Ricart Real, Xavier Romero Monio, Cristina Cruz Gomez. Photos: Amaneceres Fotograficos; **136T** Höweler + Yoon Architecture; **136B** Stewart Hollenstein; **137 (all)** Saucier + Perrotte architectes, photography: Marc Cramer and Gilles Saucier; **140** Joel Sanders Architect; **142 (all)** Courtesy Architects EAT, photo: Derek Swalwell; **143T** Courtesy Niel M. Denari Architects, Photo: Fujitsuka Mitsumasa; **143CL, CR** blank studio architecture, Bill Timmerman Photography; **143B** Joel Sanders Architect; **146** © Nigel Young / Foster + Partners; **147T** © David Nelson / Foster + Partners; **147B** © BPR / Foster + Partners; **148 (all)** © FLC/ADAGP, Paris and DACS, London 2014; **149 (all)** Sam Leist, Kingston University, London; **150** Aimee Lam, Kingston University, London; **151T** Richard Murphy Architects Ltd., Bill Black, Director; **151B** Alex Nevedomskis, Kingston University, London; **152 (all)** Laura Jackett-Simpson, Nottingham Trent University; **153TL** Letitia Vale, Nottingham Trent University; **153TR** Alex Shepherd, Kingston University, London; **153B** Jessica Chong, Emma Hancox, Jirina Kubesova, Yuet Kwan, Alex Nevedomskis, Andrew Quinn, Kingston University, London; **155** Rogers Stirk Harbour + Partners; **156** Cartlidge Levene and Studio Myerscough; **157T** Hyunjoon Yoo; **157B** courtesy Studio SKLIM; **158** COEN!; **159T** Robert M. Gurney, FAIA, Architect, project architect: Brian Tuskey; **159B** Image courtesy of LEESER Architecture; **160** By courtesy of the Trustees of Sir John Soane's Museum; **161TL** Rogers Stirk Harbour + Partners; **161C** Joel Sanders Architect, Karen van Lengen, Ben Rubin; **161B** Robert M. Gurney, FAIA, Architect; **162L** Rogers Stirk Harbour + Partners; **162R** Courtesy Dake Wells Architecture, design principal: Andrew Wells, FAIA; project architect: Mark Wheeler, AIA; photography Gayle Babcock, Architectural Imageworks, LLC; **163T** Courtesy Vir.Mueller Architects, partners: Pankaj Vir Gupta, Christine Mueller; project managers: Harsh Vardhan, Kai Pederson; project team: Sarah Gill, Saurabh Jain, Everett Hollander; drawing: Kai Pederson; **163B** Johnsen Schmaling Architects; **164T** Joel Sanders Architect; **164B** group8; **165L** Höweler + Yoon Architecture; **165R** Drawing by Nader Tehrani (NADAA, formerly Office dA) ; **166TL** NFOE et associés architectes; **166TR** Rogers Stirk Harbour + Partners; **166BL** Joel Sanders Architect; **166BR** De Leon & Primmer Architectural Workshop; **167 (all)** Oliver Corrin, Kingston University, London; **168** Illustration by Ola Rune, Claesson Koivisto Rune; **169T** courtesy Dear Design S.L., design team: Ignasi Llauradó, Eric Dufourd; **169B** Rogers Stirk Harbour + Partners; **171** Fran Silvestre Arquitectos, principles in charge, Fran Silverstre and Maria José Sàez; **172L** Robert Browes, Nottingham Trent University; **172R** Ronald Yu, Nottingham Trent University; **173** Rogers Stirk Harbour + Partners; **174** form-ula, Photography by Amy Barkow | Barkow Photo www.barkowphoto.com; **176** Copyright & Intellectual property of Kinnersley Kent Design, illustrated by Chris Jackson, Graphic Designer, Kinnersley Kent Design; **177T, CL, CR** NC-office, Elizabeth Cardona, Cristina Canton, Nikolay Nedev, Peter Nedev, Mauricio Gonzalez; **177B** Joel Sanders Architect; **178T** © Suzanne Martin; **178B, 179T, BL** Kinersley Kent Design, www.kkd.co.uk; **179BR** © Ian Higgins; **180 (all)** Design: Zemberek Design Team, Photograph: Safak Emrence; **181TL, TR** form-ula, Photography by Amy Barkow | Barkow Photo www.barkowphoto.com; **181BL** © Peter Cook / View Pictures; **181BR** Gareth Payne, Nottingham Trent University; **182** Tatjana Jakowicka, Kingston University, London

Author's acknowledgements

Much of what is contained in this book is a result of twenty-five years of teaching and thanks must go to the many hundreds of students I have worked with at Nottingham Trent University, the University of Wolverhampton, Kingston University and The Royal College of Art. All of these students, no matter their ability, have contributed to the development of my understanding of the subject. In particular much was achieved with the classes of 1993, 1995, 1996, 1997, 1999, 2000, 2002 and 2007 – thank you for working so hard!

At the start of my teaching career I was lucky to work with Peter Vickers. I thank him for the endless hours of conversation about the subject, his keen sense of irony and for being the best teacher I have ever had.

Before starting this project I had no idea about the complexities of sourcing images for publication – with over 400 images to be found and permissions secured I am truly grateful to my picture researchers James Haldane and Giulia Hetherington for all their work.

The team at Laurence King were exceptionally patient with me during the extended period before a word was written – thanks go to Philip Cooper, Liz Faber and Sara Goldsmith, and also to Kim Sinclair.

Finally thanks to Jill & Barney – without their support it would not have been possible to complete this project.